Preparing Traditional Music Manuscript

Including a Handbook of Instrumentation, Theory, and Musical Terms

Michael Mohn

M.Mohn Publishing
Fairfield, California

Preparing Traditional Music Manuscript

Published by M. Mohn Publishing
2791F N.Texas St. Suite 317
Fairfield, CA 94533-7308

Manufactured in the United States of America.

ISBN 0-9624986-0-2

First Printing: September 1987
Revised Second Edition: 1990

99 98 97 96 95 94 93 92 91 90   10 9 8 7 6 5 4 3 2

Acknowledgements

Thanks to the faculty and staff of the Music Department at the California Polytechnic State University, San Luis Obispo, for their assistance in preparing this book.

Preface

This book was written to provide to composers, copyists, and music students a useful reference for the proper preparation of music manuscript, either by manual techniques or with a computer.

Most students see printed music daily, but give little thought to the notation of musical ideas. When they prepare a manuscript themselves, the result is often full of technical errors which make the music difficult to read.

This book provides information on preparing all types of music based on the general practices used by most publishers. The text describes how to prepare a neat and technically correct manuscript which may be photoengraved from the autograph. The appendices, which contains information on instrumentation, theory, and musical terms, will become an invaluable reference for theory students and composers.

M.M.

Table of Contents

1. Supplies and Equipment

Preparing neat manuscript is a skill which can be mastered only with considerable practice. Having the proper supplies and equipment can do nothing but improve the finished product. This chapter describes the equipment used for preparing music manuscript by hand. Using a computer for preparing manuscript is beyond the scope of this book; however, the principles of notation discussed in this book apply to all manuscript whether prepared by hand or with a computer. Not all the supplies listed are essential, so one must determine just what equipment is needed for the situation. The more mechanical aids used in preparing the manuscript, the closer it will come in appearance to an actual autograph used for commercial reproduction.

Pens

The fountain pen is by far the most important piece of equipment the copyist uses. Popular pens for copying music include the *Esterbrook* pen with a #2312 or #2314B point, and the *Osmiroid* pen with a "Music Writing Point" or an "Italic Medium" point. A satisfactory pen must be able to produce both thick and thin lines, depending on the direction of the strokes.

Technical pens used by draftsmen are excellent for drawing fine lines for stems, ledger lines, slurs, and bars. For lettering performance directions and titles, the *Speedball* pen is the most widely used. A variety of points with various widths and tips are available.

Most felt tip pens are not acceptable for manuscript because the ink is too light and is not waterproof. However, there is one felt tip pen, the *Alvin* "Penstix," designed for technical drawing, that is an excellent pen for preparing manuscript. The ink is of "India Ink" density, and it is waterproof. The pen is available in three widths: 0.3mm, 0.5mm, and 0.7mm, models 3013, 3015, and 3017, respectively. The drawback of this pen is its inability to produce both thick and thin strokes.

The type of ink used is very important. It must be black; blue-black and colored inks are not acceptable. Most fountain pen inks and writing inks are too light for copying music. India ink cannot be used because it does not flow well and will clog the pen. The best ink for writing music is *Monarch Music Writing Ink*. Acceptable substitutes are *Higgins Engrossing Ink*, *Pelikan Brand Ink*, and *Cameo Brand Ink*. Drawing Ink used by draftsmen is also acceptable if the pen is emptied and cleaned after each use.

Keep the pens scrupulously clean to insure free flow of the ink, especially when using heavier inks. Wipe and blot the point frequently, and rinse it with water whenever it becomes dirty. If the pen becomes clogged with dry ink, special pen cleaning solvents are available to restore the pen.

Pencil

Pencil is not suitable for most manuscript other than rough drafts because it is not as dark as ink and because it can be smeared. Use a manuscript prepared in pencil only as a master for xerographic copying so the pencil will not smear. Mechanical pencils, such as the *Pentel* or *Sakura,* are more convenient than wood pencils, because they do not need sharpening. The lead should be no harder than "HB" to produce dark characters.

Use a sharp pencil with a hard lead for guide lines and layout marks. The lines will be very light and can be easily erased without erasing the ink.

When preparing studio music, a soft red pencil is sometimes used to mark key and meter changes with a curved bracket. This can only be done if the music will not be duplicated.

For proofreading use a hard light blue pencil. The blue marks on the paper will not show up on reproductions.

Rulers and Guides

A ruler is indispensable for drawing straight lines. A 12-inch clear plastic ruler is probably the most con-venient. The edge of the ruler must be raised to avoid blotting the ink; strips of masking tape or cork can be applied to the back of flat rulers to raise the edge. For drawing bars on large scores, a 16-inch metal ruler is handy; the metal edge will remain smooth longer than a plastic one. In addition to serving as a straight edge, the ruler can be used to lay out meas-ures of equal size, as illustrated below.

For drawing stems, beams, bars, and any other short lines, a small 30°- 60°- 90° triangle is handy. Hold the triangle with only the bottom edge touching the page so that the ink does not smear.

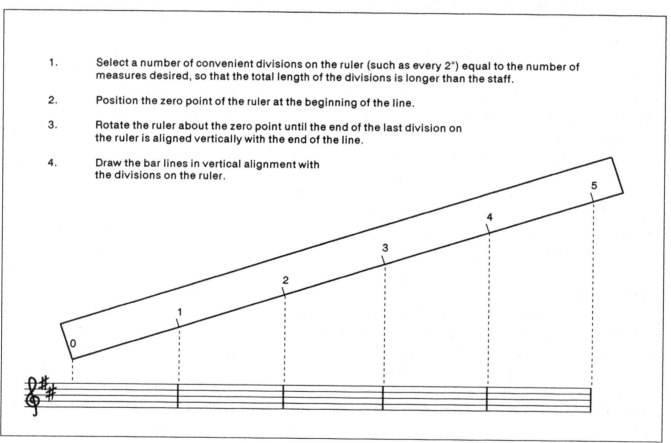

1. Select a number of convenient divisions on the ruler (such as every 2") equal to the number of measures desired, so that the total length of the divisions is longer than the staff.

2. Position the zero point of the ruler at the beginning of the line.

3. Rotate the ruler about the zero point until the end of the last division on the ruler is aligned vertically with the end of the line.

4. Draw the bar lines in vertical alignment with the divisions on the ruler.

Using the ruler to divide a staff into equal size measures.

A French curve is used to draw slurs that are too long to be drawn freehand. Because most French curves are flat, masking tape or cork "feet" must be placed on the back of the curve to raise the edge so the ink does not blot.

A lettering guide is useful for laying out guide lines for hand lettering. The guide is a plastic triangle with holes drilled in it to accept a pencil point. To draw guide lines, insert a hard pencil into a hole and slide the triangle along a ruler. Erase the lines after the ink lettering is dry.

Lettering Supplies

A good alternative to hand lettering titles and other directions is to use dry transfer lettering. These are acetate sheets containing letters and symbols which are rubbed onto the paper. Similar to dry transfer lettering is *Kroy* lettering. The *Kroy* machine prints letters onto clear tape which is then applied to the paper.

A rubber stamp set containing performance directions and the names of all the instruments can save considerable time on large copying jobs.

A typewriter with a carbon ribbon is good for lettering vocal texts. The typewriter aids in alignment of words in different parts, and the typeface avoids confusion of the text with hand-lettered directions.

Correcting Mistakes

Mistakes are inevitable when preparing manuscript. If the mistake is in pencil, use a soft white eraser like the *Staedtler Mars* Eraser for Paper and Film. Ordinary pink erasers tend to discolor the paper.

The white eraser may be used for erasing ink. Rub lightly and do not hurry the results. Ink may also be scraped off the paper with a razor blade. Smooth the resulting rough surface with the white eraser. Because the rough surface will tend to feather the ink, write the correction first; then remove the mistake by scraping.

An easier method for correction is to use a correction fluid like *Liquid Paper*. Dab the fluid over the mistake with the brush in the cap. Do not brush the fluid on because it may dissolve the ink and make the mistake worse. A problem with correction fluid is that ink may be too light when applied over it; to avoid this, draw the correction first, and then delete the ink around the correction.

For deleting large errors, *Avery* Self Adhesive Correction Tape is handy. The white paper tape, available in several widths, is simply applied over the error. Rule in any staff lines and correct the mistake on the tape. The tape may also be used to blank out unused staves on a score or in a part, and it may be used for simple bindings.

For larger mistakes splice in a new area of paper. Either glue a strip of paper in place with rubber cement or a glue stick, such as the *Faber Castell* "Uhu Stic," or cut away part of the page and tape a new piece of paper in place with correction tape or cellophane tape. If splicing is not practical, recopy the entire page.

Manuscript Paper

Manuscript paper is made in a wide variety of types and sizes. Selection of a particular size and type must be determined by the application. Be sure the paper has a smooth, hard surface so the ink will not feather. Also, use only white paper for xerographic copying.

Paper is available with either blank staves or rulings for various combinations of instruments and voices. In addition to being pre-ruled, some large score papers have four measures per line ruled in. Using pre-ruled papers whenever possible can save considerable time. Keep a few sheets of blank paper on hand for use as title pages and for hand ruling single line percussion parts.

White Paper. Several sizes of white manuscript paper have become standard over the years. White paper is available in various weights, color shades, and rulings.

Concert size paper measures 9¼ by 12½ inches. It is usually available with 10, 12, or 16 blank staves per page, or with 5 or 6 piano staves pre-ruled on each page. For most work, the 10-staff paper gives ample room between staves for performance directions. 12-staff paper is good for preparing 3 and 4 line scores.

Paper for choral work usually measures 7 by 10 inches. It is called *octavo size,* and it is available with either blank staves or with various rulings of choir, piano, and organ staves.

Marching band size paper is designed for use on music clips called lyres which are attached to marching band instruments. It measures 5½ by 6 inches, and has various numbers of blank staves.

Scores are usually written on *symphonic size* paper, measuring 10½ by 13½ inches. Blank paper is available with 14, 18, 20, and 24 staves. Various rulings for band and orchestra can be found, with or without measures drawn in. Papers which are 12½ by 19½ inches and larger with up to 60 staves can be found, either blank or with rulings for large ensembles.

Vellum. Vellum, or onion skin paper, is required when the diazo process will be used for reproduction. Modern xerographic equipment has largely replaced the diazo process. However, some composers and smaller publishing houses still use vellum; so one should be aware of the technicalities when using vellum, in case its use is ever required.

Vellum is translucent, with the staff lines printed on the back side. Using a heavy ink is essential to produce lines which will reproduce. Corrections may only be made by scraping the ink off the paper or by cutting out a section and splicing in a new piece with clear tape. Correction fluids and strips of tape glued over a mistake cannot be used.

Paper for Xerographic Copying. With the increasing use of xerographic equipment to duplicate music, using 8½ by 11, 8½ by 14, and 11 by 17 inch papers for most manuscripts will simplify duplication. Several rulings of 8½ by 11 inch paper are available. Ten-staff paper is ideal for most manuscript, and twelve-staff paper is handy for 3 and 4 line scores.

If an appropriate pre-ruled paper cannot be found for a manuscript, a custom ruling may be prepared using xerographic equipment. For example, a good piano part can be ruled by blanking out every third line of 12-staff paper with correction tape. The tape will usually not produce shadows on a good xerographic copier; if it does, cover the shadow line with correction fluid. For custom scores, make a paste-up of the ruling and copy it onto 8½ by 14 or 11 by 17 inch paper. Check that the paper used for copying is of high quality so the ink will not feather.

2. Basic Notation

This chapter discusses calligraphy and basic notation common to all types of music, both instrumental and vocal. The points illustrated on single staff lines usually apply to double-staff lines and full scores as well. Special notation for specific instruments is discussed in the next chapter. The term *studio music*, used throughout this book, refers to music written for the theater, nightclub, and entertainment industry, where the music is performed with little or no rehearsal.

Lettering

Use plain block letters for lettering on music. For titles and names, Roman lettering, Gothic lettering, or dry transfer lettering are all acceptable. Write tempo indications in small gothic letters. Write all other directions in small italic lettering.

TITLE

Allegro   *stringendo*

Always use guide lines when lettering; erase the lines after the lettering is inked. Although styles will vary, try to use the block lettering developed by draftsmen.

ABCDEFGHIJKLMNOPQRSTUVWXYZ
aabcdefgghijklmnopqrstuv wxyz
1234567890

For clarity, draw the capital I, lower-case l, and numeral 1 as shown. To avoid confusion with the 4,

draw the 9 as an upside-down 6.

The placement of words is very important. Write tempo indications and directions above the staff. All other writing goes below the staff except in vocal music.

Dynamics and directions are written between the staves in a double-staff line.

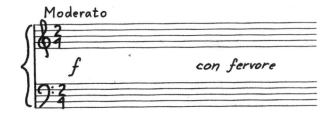

Clef Signs

Draw clef signs as they appear in engraved music; avoid extra frills and florid swirls. The clef signs in common use are the treble clef, bass clef, alto clef, and tenor clef. There is considerable variation among handwritten clefs. Practice drawing them until they can be drawn easily. Avoid using archaic clef signs that are sometimes seen in British music.

Key Signatures

Write key signatures according to the traditional pattern.

In contemporary music the key signature is often left out, and accidentals are used in front of the notes as needed. Usually, the normal convention of an accidental carrying through an entire measure will apply. If the accidental is to apply only to the note before which it appears, include a notation at the beginning of the work describing the convention being used.

Meter Signatures

Place meter signatures directly after the key signature, or directly after the clef sign if no key signature is used. The numbers are placed within the confines of the staff.

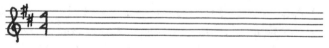

In scores with many meter changes, oversize figures are often written to make it easier for the conductor to see the meter changes.

Place the meter signature only on the first line of the music, unless it changes later in the manuscript. Use common time and cut time symbols only if there is no meter change in the piece.

When preparing studio music, use the clef sign only on the first line, and draw a curved bracket to the right of the key signature.

Clef, Key, and Meter Changes

The examples below show how to change clefs, keys, and meters within the measure and at the end of the line.

Bar Lines

Use bar lines to mark off measures and, at the beginning of a score, to connect the staves. A single line staff does not have a bar line at the beginning except in studio music. Draw bar lines with a ruler, perpendicular to the staff, from the top line to the bottom line. The width of the line is twice that of a staff line. Draw a double bar as two parallel lines spaced one-half the width between two staff lines. A double bar at the end of a piece is drawn with a narrow bar line and a wide bar line; the width of the wide line is one-half the spacing of two staff lines. Draw bar lines continuously through both staves of a double-staff line.

Note Heads

Three types of note heads are used in music: the open note head, the closed note head, and the whole note. The note head should be large enough to fill the space between two lines. The shape of a note head is oval, slanting upward to the right.

Draw open note heads with two strokes of the fountain pen, or as a continuous circle with the technical pen. The solid note head is simply an open note head with an additional stroke to fill in the center. Draw whole notes slightly larger than normal, with the pen held at a different angle to achieve a different shading. The note must be shaded with additional strokes if drawn with the technical pen.

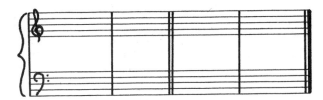

open: *closed:*   *whole note:*

Practice writing note heads until they are consistent in size and shape.

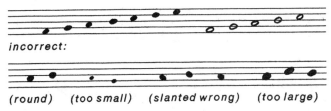

correct:

incorrect:

(round)   (too small)   (slanted wrong)   (too large)

Draw cue notes and grace notes smaller than regular notes, but with the same shape and consistency. They are usually drawn with the technical pen and are not shaded.

Ledger Lines and Octave Sign

Ledger lines are needed if the notes exceed the limits of the staff. The lines are the same width as staff lines, and they are spaced the same distance apart as the staff lines. Every note requires its own set of ledger lines, and the ledger lines must be long enough to accommodate the note head. For neatness and accuracy, use the ruler to draw all ledger lines.

correct: *incorrect:*

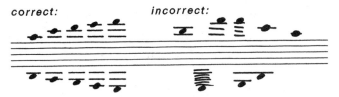

Ledger lines for cues are proportionately smaller, but the spacing between them remains the same.

In scores with limited space for ledger lines, or in some keyboard music, the sign *8* or *8va* is used above the staff to show that the notes are played one octave higher than written. Place a broken line above the passage, and mark the end of the transposition with a short vertical bracket. After an especially long transposition, add the term *loco*.

A transposition of two octaves is similar, but use the sign *15* or *15ma* instead of *8*. For three octaves, the correct sign is *22da*. If the transposition is to be one octave lower than written, place the sign *8va* or *8va bassa* below the staff.

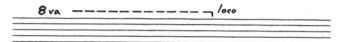

Stems

Draw stems as thin lines the same width as that of a staff line. Be sure that they touch the note head in the proper place. Attempting to draw stems and notes together in a single stroke results in sloppy work. The stem usually extends for one octave. Place it on the right side of the note if it goes up, and on the left side if it goes down.

For single notes, the stem goes down for notes on or above the third line and up for notes below the third line. The note on the third line may be stemmed up, on occasion, when surrounded on both sides by stems up notes, as shown below.

Other exceptions to stem directions for single notes are discussed in the sections on beams, divided parts, grace notes, and cues. When the notes are placed on ledger lines, lengthen the stems to extend into the staff at least two lines.

Flags and Beams

Flags are used for single eighth notes, sixteenth notes, and smaller value notes. Draw the flag as a curved hook and place it on the right side of the stem, regardless of the stem direction. Lengthen the stem for each additional flag that is added. If the note is on ledger lines, the flags must be contained within the staff.

Use beams to link together notes of less than a quarter note duration. Application of beams is discussed in the section on notating rhythms. Draw beams as heavy lines one-half the width of a space between two staff lines. Space multiple beams the same distance apart as the staff lines. Lengthen the stems for each additional beam, and extend the stems through all the beams.

Beam the notes so the majority of the stems are in the correct direction.

If the stems could go either way, point them down.

If one note is far removed from the rest, it often sets the beam direction regardless of the other notes.

Slant the beams to follow the contour of the music. The beams are horizontal if the grouping starts and ends on the same note.

When notes of differing value are beamed together, short beams are used in the grouping. Place the short beam on the right side of the stem at the beginning of a group, and on the left side for all successive short notes.

When notes are on ledger lines, the beams must be contained within the staff.

If wide skips occur in the music, the notes may be beamed as follows:

Rests

Rests are usually drawn with the fountain pen. If drawn with the technical pen, the rest must be shaded to have the same appearance.

Place the whole rest under the fourth line in the center of the measure. Use the whole rest to indicate a full measure of rest regardless of the metric length of the measure. The half rest is the same size as the whole rest, but it is placed above the third line. Draw the quarter rest in the same way that it is engraved. The rest is drawn from bottom to top in one continuous stroke of the fountain pen.

Never use any of the following variants of the quarter rest:

incorrect:

Draw rests of a quarter duration or less with curved hooks and a connecting stem. The example shows the correct placement of eighth, sixteenth, thirty-second, and sixty-fourth rests.

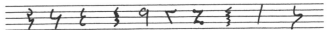

If the music has two or more bars of rest in succession, use a multiple bar rest. Draw the multiple bar rest as a heavy bar on the third line with the number of measures included in the rest centered over the bar. The multiple bar rest cannot be used in a score, but it can be used in parts extracted from the score.

correct: *incorrect:*

On a double-staff system place the multiple bar rest on both staves.

Avoid using the archaic system of multiple bar rests shown below. If recopying old parts, use modern multiple bar rests in their place.

Time Dots

Time dots are placed after notes and rests as shown in the example below. The use of time dots is explained in the section on notating rhythm.

Accessory Numbers

When there is a deviation from the normal division of the beat, show the change with an accessory number. On beamed figures, place the number above or below the beam. Do not place a slur over the number unless the notes are to be slurred.

If the notes are not beamed, or if the figure includes rests, use a square bracket to enclose the fig-

ure. Place the bracket below the notes if all the stems are down. If one or more stems go up, place the bracket above the notes.

In instances where there is not enough room for the accessory numbers on the stem side of the notes, place them above or below the note heads.

If the same borrowed figure is repeated many times in succession, use the auxiliary number for only the first two or three groupings.

Chords and Divided Parts

When more than one note in a group is played by the same performer, the note group is called a *chord*. If each note of the grouping is played by a different person, it is called a *divided part* or a *divisi*.

If all the sounding pitches are of the same value, they are all stemmed together. The direction of the stem is selected based on the largest interval and the number of notes above or below the third line. In a beamed figure, the largest intervals of the entire beamed group determines the direction of all the stems.

In cases where the stems might go either direction, point them down.

Write seconds in ascending order. If the chord contains many seconds, place as many note heads as possible on the correct side of the stem.

If independent motion of two parts is written on the same line, use separate sets of stems.

If a unison exists in a split-stem part, place two stems on the same note head.

Avoid the common error found on many split-stem parts.

Open note heads cannot share a stem with closed note heads Write both notes.

When the stems are split, write seconds in reverse (descending) order, unless the voices are crossed, to give better stem placement.

When two players share a staff, as is common in instrumental scores, show entrances and exits of the parts clearly. If both parts are the same, place the term *a2* above the staff.

If a single part is divided, with half the players in the section playing one line and the other half playing the other, place the term *div.* where the parts divide and the term *unis.* where they come together again.

If one or two players are to play a part with the rest of the players resting, use the term *solo* or *one desk* to indicate one player or two players, respectively. When the rest of the players are to join in, place the term *tutti* above the line.

If the dynamics or articulation of a split-stem part is different for each part, write directions both above and below the staff.

Do not double rests in split-stem parts if the rhythm is obvious.

If the parts contain independent rests, place the rests off-center to allow room for the second part. Whole and half rests may be placed on ledger lines above or below the staff if necessary. Keep the rests aligned with the beat except for the whole rest, which is always centered in the measure.

Slurs and Ties

Use slurs to show a legato passage. On a wind instrument, the player will play the slurred notes without interrupting the column of air. A string player will play the notes with a single bow stroke. The keyboard player will connect the notes as smoothly as possible. Place slurs above the staff unless all the stems are up. The start and end of the slur is even with the center of the note head.

Split-stem parts require two slurs.

Chords and parts with shared stems require only one slur for all the notes.

Show slurs past the end of the line clearly.

Do not break slurs in half, but extend them the full length of the slurred passage.

incorrect: *correct:*

Use a tie to connect two notes of equal pitch to produce one longer note. Place the tie for a single voice at the heads of the notes, and curve it opposite the stem direction. More than two notes tied together in a row require a tie from one head to the next, otherwise, each note will be articulated as if the passage were slurred.

Show ties past the end of the line clearly.

In chords all tied notes must have ties. Place the ties relative to the third line of the staff. If all the notes are high or low, balance the ties. If the chord contains a tied second, the tie for the second must be opposite, no matter where it is on the staff.

Draw ties combined with slurs correctly. Study the following example carefully.

incorrect:

correct:

In legato chord progressions place the slurs and ties to avoid confusion with one another.

incorrect:

correct:

Accidentals

Accidental signs are used to change the pitch of a single note, or all the notes within a single measure. Draw the sharp with four strokes, first two downward thin lines; then two upward-slanting thick lines. Draw the flat and natural signs with two strokes. Draw the double flat sign as two flat signs placed side by side. The double sharp can be drawn in four ways. The first is the way it appears engraved; the next three are acceptable in manuscript.

sharp:	flat:	natural:	double flat:	double sharp:
♯	♭	♮	♭♭	𝄪 ✕ ✕ ❈

Draw accidental signs carefully. The following variants are incorrect:

incorrect:

Draw accidentals on the line or space directly in front of the note they affect. They must not touch the note, a ledger line, or each other, nor can they be drawn too large.

correct: *incorrect:*

If an accidental is inadvertently left out and there is not enough space to place it properly, recopy the part. The accidental cannot be written in above the note.

incorrect:

The next example shows the guidelines for placing accidentals on chords.

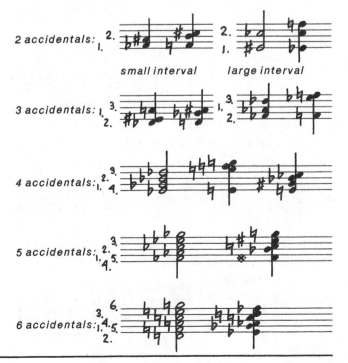

The practice of canceling old accidentals is no longer used.

incorrect:

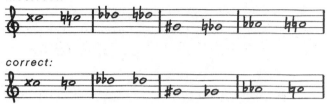

correct:

Traditionally, an accidental on one pitch does not affect the other octaves; however, many publishers are using one accidental to affect all pitches. If there is any doubt about the proper pitch, use an accidental for clarity.

Accidentals are cancelled by a bar line unless carried over to the next note by a tie. If the next note following the tied note is to be of the same pitch, use an accidental again. For clarity place a natural sign on the following note if it is not to be altered.

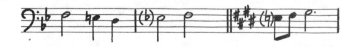

Placing reminder accidentals in parenthesis in the measure following a key change, and in a measure following an altered measure is helpful to the performer.

When notating chords and multiple voice lines which will be played by one player, the accidental need only be stated once, no matter how the voices may cross. If two players are sharing the part on a single line, however, repeat the accidentals in each voice.

In contemporary twelve-tone music with no key signature, an accidental sign is often placed before every note. A note at the beginning of the piece should explain this convention. The note should also say whether or not the accidental applies only to the note which it precedes, or to all the notes in the measure.

Tremolos, Trills, and Tremolandos

Tremolos are played by repeating a note over and over again a definite number of times per beat for a measured tremolo, and as fast as possible for an unmeasured tremolo. A trill is played by alternating rapidly between the given note and the note an interval of a second higher. A tremolando is similar to a trill, except the interval is greater than a second. Tremolandos may be measured or unmeasured.

Write a tremolo by drawing a short segment of beam through the stem of a note or beneath a whole note. If the tremolo is measured, write out the first beat. An unmeasured tremolo has three lines, and often the term *trem.* is placed at the beginning of the passage.

Write a thirty-second note measured tremolo with an *8* above the first note to avoid confusion with the unmeasured tremolo.

Split-stem parts require tremolo indications above and below the staff.

Double bowing and double tonguing are usually notated using tremolo signs. Place the tremolo sign parallel to the note beam.

Two tremolo signs placed on a beamed figure indicate an unmeasured tremolo for the duration of each note.

The trill is indicated by placing the term *tr* over the note. If the trill is over a long note or extends over several tied notes, add a wavy line over the duration of the trill.

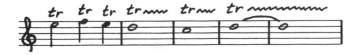

A trilled note is assumed to be the next diatonic pitch above the given note as determined by the key of the music, unless notated otherwise.

If a trill is to have an ornament at the end, write the auxiliary notes out as grace notes. If the trill begins on an auxiliary note, place the grace note before the trill.

Tremolandos are written like tremolos, but with both the upper and lower pitches written out, both notes showing the time value of the tremolando, and with the beams placed between the notes. For half note tremolandos, attach one beam to the stem. Write out tremolandos of less than quarter note value. Unmeasured tremolandos have a total of three beams.

A measured tremolando has one or two beams. Write out the first beat.

Repeat Signs, Codas, and Endings

Repeat signs are used to save time when writing out a part. Single measure repeats may be used in an individual part, while section repeats, codas, and endings must be used in all parts of an ensemble.

Use repeats within a measure only in rhythm parts in studio music. Do not use them in traditional music except in a rough draft. Show a repeat of a beamed figure with a diagonal beam for each repetition. Show chord repeats by drawing the stems of the repeated notes.

Draw repeats of a single measure as a thick diagonal line and two dots. Number multiple repetitions with the written measure being number one.

Draw a two measure repeat as two diagonal lines with two dots and the figure 2 placed on a bar line. Do not use an abbreviation to repeat three or more measures.

On a double-staff system, draw the repeat signs on both staves.

Use repeat signs correctly and with discretion. Write out whole notes and very simple patterns rather than using repeat signs. Avoid the use of the single and double measure repeat signs altogether in classical music.

incorrect:

Do not write more than eight repeated measures on a line, or begin a line with a repeat sign. To begin a new line, write the measure again and begin numbering the repeats over again.

Do not use repeats with overlapping slurs, as in the following example. Write the passage out properly.

incorrect:

Arrangers often use a short cut that should not be copied for a player.

incorrect:

Never combine a two measure repeat with a single measure repeat or a rest.

incorrect:

Repeats of entire sections of music are used frequently. The repeats are drawn as follows:

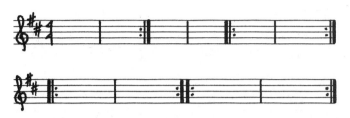

Show endings with brackets placed above the measure.

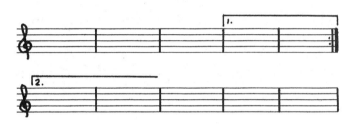

Never hide a repeat sign inside the second ending. Instead, place another ending at the end of the next section.

incorrect:

correct:

The following examples illustrate the notation for a *Da Capo* and a *Dal Segno*.

Da Capo with a Coda:

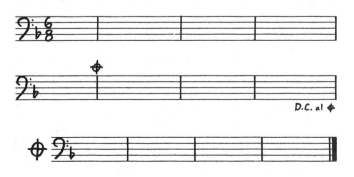

Da Capo:

Dal Segno with a Coda:

Dal Segno:

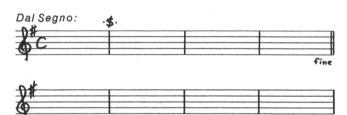

In studio music make repeat signs more noticeable.

Place directions such as 3 x's (play three times) and 2 x.o. (play second time only), found frequently in studio music, above the staff, where applicable.

Notation of Rhythms

The proper notation of rhythm is best learned by example, as there are few actual rules to follow. The key to notating rhythms properly is to make them clear and easy to read.

Beamed figures often have broken secondary beams to show division of the beats and specific articulation. Beams may occasionally be combined with flagged notes to emphasize articulation or dynamics.

Use beams to show unusual groupings of notes in asymmetric meters. If the pattern changes frequently in a fast tempo, numbers are sometimes used to help the performer see the division. Occasionally, beams are extended over bar lines.

Irregular divisions of notes are notated correctly as follows:

simple meter:

compound meter:

Rhythmic Notation of Simple Meter

The following examples show nearly every conceivable simple meter rhythm. In general, when writing a measure in simple meter, do not carry a note, beam, or rest across the middle of the measure except in simple rhythms and syncopation. Do not use dotted rests except the dotted eighth rest.

Simple Rhythms (4/4 meter).

Simple Rhythms (3/4 meter).

Simple Rhythms (2/4 meter).

Beamed Figures (4/4 meter). Use beams to divide a measure in halves or quarters. Never extend a beam to include a rest, as in the second example.

Beamed Figures (3/4 meter). Each beat in triple meter should be clearly seen. Be careful not to write 6/8 figures.

incorrect:

correct:

Rests (4/4 meter). The general rule for rests is that a note (other than a single sixteenth note) should not be immediately followed by a rest of longer duration to complete the quarter measure.

incorrect:

correct:

Rests (3/4 meter). In triple meter the half rest is not used; and the whole rest is used to show a full measure of rest.

incorrect:

correct:

Augmentation.

incorrect:

correct:

Syncopation. In syncopated rhythms the half measure must be clear except in the simplest cases.

incorrect:

correct:

incorrect:

correct:

Borrowed Division.

incorrect:

correct:

Complex Rhythms. A correctly notated complex rhythm should divide the measure into halves and quarters.

incorrect

correct:

incorrect

correct:

Rhythmic Notation of Compound Meter

In general, when writing in compound meter, show every beat clearly. Do not use dotted rests, with the exception of the dotted eighth, unless writing in 9/8 or 12/8 meter.

Simple Rhythms.

Beamed Figures.
Use beams to divide the measures into beats. Never extend a beam to include a rest.

Rests.
Use the whole rest to show one measure of rest in any compound meter. Use dotted rests only in 9/8 and 12/8 meter.

Augmentation.

Syncopation. In compound meter retain the distinct beats in a measure except in the simplest cases.

Borrowed Division.

Complex Rhythms. When writing complex rhythms, be careful to maintain the compound meter and not write simple meter figures.

Notation of Mixed Meter

If the meter changes every measure in a repeated pattern, place the pattern of meters at the beginning as if it were one meter signature.

If a piece is written in simple meter with a frequent and random change to its equivalent compound meter, place the compound meter in parenthesis in the meter signature.

Notation of Asymmetric Meter

Asymmetric meters, such as 5/4 and 7/4 are composed of groups of the simple meters 2/4 and 3/4 in different combinations. 5/4 meters must be written consistently divided into 2/4 + 3/4 or 3/4 + 2/4. 7/4 is divided into either 4/4 + 3/4 or 3/4 + 4/4. Both meters may be written out as a mixed meter (see above). If the division is hard to see, place subdivision dots in the measure. A pitch played for a full measure requires a tie, and the notes used should retain the correct metric pattern; do not use a dotted whole note or variations of the whole note. Use a whole rest to show a full measure of rest.

Spacing

Space the notes in a passage in proportion to their length.

Place the whole note at the beginning of the measure, and center a whole rest in the middle.

Place other value rests exactly where their corresponding notes would be placed.

Give dotted notes a little more space, and space sixteenth notes more closely together.

Make allowances for accidentals.

The length of measures depends on what the measure contains. In individual parts, rule equal length measures only if they all contain the same note values. In scores, pre-ruled measures can be used to save time, but only if all the notes will fit neatly into a measure. Obviously, a measure of 32 thirty-second notes needs more space than a measure of 1 whole note.

Alignment

Alignment of notes applies to divided parts, two-staff systems, and scores. The following example shows proper alignment in a double-staff system. In general, align note heads vertically with one another and with the beat or fraction of the beat.

When chords containing seconds are involved, align the notes on the correct side of the stem. When two chords on the same staff are separated by a second, the chords are offset.

When a clef changes in one staff of a score, space the other staves to maintain alignment of the beats.

Grace Notes

Use grace notes to show ornaments in music. The grace notes are played just before the beat, or just before the note which they are joined to. In music from the classic period, single grace notes were often used instead of appoggiaturas; write out the figure without using a grace note when copying such music.

Write grace notes and their stems, beams, and accidentals smaller than normal size notes. The stems point up, except on the lower voice of a divided part. The grace notes are slurred together, unless they are to be articulated separately. Write a single grace note as an eighth note with a slash through the flag. Beam two grace notes together as sixteenth notes; write three or more grace notes as thirty-second notes. Do not include the metric value of the grace notes in the meter of the measure.

Cues

Cue notes are written into parts for one of two purposes: to cue a player following a long period of rest, or to allow a player to cover an important part of another instrument which may be missing. Write cue notes for transposing instruments in the proper key for the instrument reading the cues. For example, a clarinet player should be able to produce the proper pitches when playing flute cues. At the beginning of the cues, write the name of the instrument whose part is cued. All the cues are either stemmed up with whole rests placed below them, or stemmed down, with whole rests placed above them.

A cue after a long period of rest should be a part that the player would clearly hear, such as the melody line, or an earlier entrance of a nearby player.

A cue for an important part must show all the articulation and dynamics of the original part. Show this type of cue in the score as well as in the part. The example below shows how an oboe solo would look in a clarinet part.

Performance Directions

Directions are notated in music with both words and symbols. This section discusses indications for tempo, style, ornaments, dynamics, fermatas, pauses, and glissando effects.

Place tempo indications above the staff, beginning after the bar at which they take effect. Capitalize the first letter of the first word, and do not use a period. A style indication may be included if it applies to the entire section. A metronome marking may be placed in parenthesis after the words.

Write style indications not included with the tempo using small italics below the staff at the places where they apply.

The ornament symbols understood by most musicians are the *turn, mordent,* and *inverted mordent.* Write out any other ornaments in the part using grace notes. The following example illustrates the three ornament symbols and their chromatic alterations.

Changes in dynamics and tempo are notated using both words and symbols. The frequently used notations are given below.

ppp	pianississimo
pp	pianissimo
p	piano
mp	mezzo-piano
mf	mezzo-forte
f	forte
ff	fortissimo
fff	fortississimo
fp	forte-piano
sfz	sforzando
<	crescendo (cresc.)
>	diminuendo (dim.)
poco a poco	little by little
e	and
rit.	ritardando
rall.	rallentando
accel.	accelerando

Place directions under the staff just before the note they affect. Place the sforzando and forte-piano directly below a note. Crescendos and diminuendos must start and end accurately.

Place articulation markings at the heads of the notes, except in split-stem parts, where they are placed at the stems. Place the markings inside slurs and ties, and if more than one is used on a note, place them in the order shown.

The fermata shows an indefinite sustaining of a note. Center it over a note. Place the fermata upside down below a note only in a moving split-stem part. Never place the fermata in the confines of the staff.

Show pauses in music with the breath mark for a very short pause, the luftpause (sometimes called "train tracks") for a longer break, or the general pause (sometimes called a "grand pause") for a very long break. Place the pause marking in all the parts of ensemble music.

Show glissando effects with a wavy line. Add the terms *gliss.*, *rip*, *smear*, or *fall off* if needed to clarify the meaning of the sign.

Rehearsal Numbers

Rehearsal numbers aid in ensemble playing by providing easily found starting points within a work, other than at the beginning of a major section. There are many systems of rehearsal numbers; each has good and bad points.

Every measure may be numbered below the staff after each bar line.

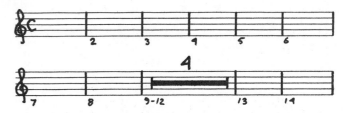

A measure number may be placed at the beginning of each line.

A measure number may be placed in a box at evenly spaced intervals, such as every ten measures.

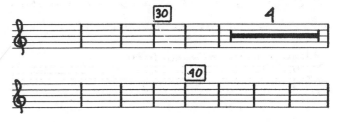

A measure number may be placed in a box at strategic locations, such as key changes or just before a difficult passage.

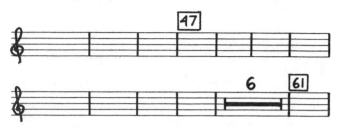

Consecutive numbers or letters may be placed in a box at evenly spaced intervals.

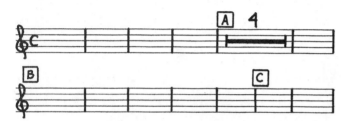

Consecutive numbers or letters may be placed in a box at strategic locations.

No matter what system is used, be sure to include all the rehearsal numbers in all the parts. For example, if the flutes have 17 measures of rest, but there is a rehearsal number after eight measures, write the part as shown below.

3. Special Notation

In addition to the basic notation discussed in the previous chapter, there is a variety of symbols and procedures which apply only to specific instruments or voice. This chapter discusses the special notation used for wind instruments, strings, percussion, keyboard instruments, harp, guitar and rhythm instruments, and vocal music.

Wind Instruments

Included in the topic of wind instruments are all the woodwinds and brass. Write wind instrument parts on single staff lines. If the instrument is transposing, write the part transposed into the proper key. Write high and low notes on the proper ledger lines, rather than using the octave sign.

Articulation. All single notes played by a wind instrument will be articulated by a technique called *tonguing*. Several degrees of smoothness may be notated, from staccato to slurring.

Several types of accents may be written using the accent sign, the marcato sign, and other dynamic signs. A special accent called the *bell tone*, which imitates the sound of a bell, can be specified for brass instruments. The horn can produce a harsh, brassy tone by overblowing the stopped horn, as shown by the term *stopped* with + signs over the notes.

Write fast articulated passages and tremolos only within the limits of the players. Brass players and flute players can use a technique called *double tonguing* to tongue sixteenth notes at a speed as fast as 152 beats per minute. Reed players cannot double tongue; about the fastest a good reed player can tongue is sixteenth notes at a tempo of 90 beats per minute.

To compensate for the reed player's inability to tongue notes very fast, an articulation of slurring two notes then tonguing two notes is often written in fast passages. Many reed players will use this articulation even if it is not written. Another technique is to split the section in half; each half alternates playing one or two beats while the other half rests.

Notate a very rapid tonguing, called *flutter tonguing*, by writing tremolos with the added term *flutter*, followed by a wavy line above the notes.

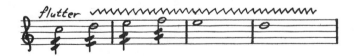

Mutes. Using the mute in brass instruments is shown by the term *con sordino* or *with mute* placed above the staff. Place the term *senza sordino* or *open* above the staff at the end of the muted passage. Allow a short period of rest before a muted passage to give the player time to put the mute into the bell. The player will use a straight mute unless another type of mute is specified.

Special Effects. Place directions for special effects above the staff. If the effect produces a pitch, notate the pitches using the correct notes. Use diamond and x-shaped notes and wavy lines to show relative pitches.

String Instruments

String instruments include the violin, viola, cello, and bass. The harp and guitar are discussed in their own sections. Write string parts on single lines. On occasion, the violin part may split to a braced part for clarity. Write high notes with ledger lines, rather than using the octave sign.

Bowing. Unless marked otherwise, all notes will be played with the bow. If stating the direction of the bow is necessary, place a square bracket above a note to begin at the frog, and a v-shaped sign above a note to begin at the tip of the bow. All the notes under a slur will be played in one bow. If a passage is to be played on only one string, place the indication above the staff.

A legato bowing effect called *louré* is notated using tenuto lines under a slur.

Show staccato and spicatto bowing with dots at the note heads. Show heavier staccato with a wedge symbol. Staccato dots enclosed by a slur can indicate either a group of staccato notes played with one bow, an arpeggio across all the strings, or a *jeté*.

Show the technique of alternating from an open string to a string stopped at the same pitch by splitting the stems and placing a small circle above the pitches played on the open string.

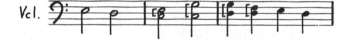

If two notes are played at the same time, write them with a bracket in front of the notes to distinguish them from a divided part.

Pizzicato. If a passage is to be plucked rather than bowed, place the term *pizz.* above the staff. When the pizzicato section is over, the term *arco* shows that the bow is used again. A very powerful pizzicato, where the string is plucked so hard that it snaps against the fingerboard, is notated with a special sign.

Notate pizzicato played with the left hand at the fingerboard with small cross signs.

Mutes. Using the mute on string instruments is indicated by the term *con sordino* or "with mute" placed above the staff. Use the term *senza sordino* or "without mute" at the end of the muted passage. Allow a short period of rest before a muted section to give a player time to install the mute.

Special Effects. Write directions for special effects above the staff. The common indications using the bow are *sul tasto* or "over the fingerboard," *sul ponticello* or "near the bridge," *col legno* or "with the wood," and *apunte d'arco* or "at the point of the bow." Return to normal bowing with the indication *modo ordinario* or "ordinary way." Describe other effects specifically. Use diamond and x-shaped note heads if the effect does not produce a pitch.

The natural harmonic is a pitch one octave higher than the written note. Notate it with a small circle above the written note. Additional harmonics occur at an interval of two octaves above the written note, and a twelfth above the written note. Write these harmonics by placing a diamond shaped note head a perfect fourth or perfect fifth above the written note, and the actual sounding note in parenthesis two octaves or a twelfth above the written note.

Percussion

The percussion can be divided into two groups: definite pitch instruments, like the xylophone and tympani, and indefinite pitch instruments, like the bass drum and triangle. Preparing a studio part for the trap set is discussed in the section on guitar and rhythm instruments.

Key Signatures. Use key signatures for all the definite pitch instruments except the tympani.

Clef Signs. Write parts for definite pitch instruments on a normal staff, using the proper clef sign: bass clef for the tympani, and treble clef for the mallet instruments. Write parts for indefinite pitch instruments using a neutral clef sign, either on a normal staff or on a single line. Indefinite pitch instruments such as the tom toms and temple blocks are shown on a single staff, with relative pitches notated on different lines.

Instruments. Frequently, one player will play several different instruments. Write the changes in instrumentation above the staff as soon as it is possible for the player to change instruments. State the clef and key signature for the new instrument, if needed, at the time of the change. Sometimes two different instruments are played at the same time; write and label the parts like a split-stem part.

On a tympani part state the tuning of the tympani from low to high at the beginning of the music. If it is necessary to change the tuning of a note, allow time for the tympanist to make the change, and note the change above the staff as soon as it is possible for the player to make the change. Write glissando effects to show the beginning and ending pitches.

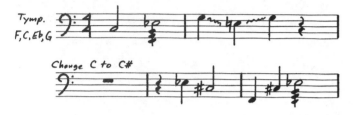

If no directions for sticks are indicated, the percussionist will use ordinary sticks or mallets. Write directions to use special sticks above the staff.

Notation. The part for a percussion instrument will be played as written. Write flams, drags, and other figures accurately with grace notes.

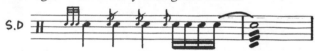

Occasionally, diamond and x-shaped notes are used for cymbal parts. In most cases, however, use standard notes unless there is a good reason to use other symbols for clarity. Do not use a picture depicting a triangle and beater for a triangle part.

To show continuing vibration of cymbals and other instruments which ring, place a short slur over the note. The note value should be as long as practical, as it makes no sense to call for a note to ring, then follow it immediately by rests. The abbreviation *L.V.* (*laissez vibrer*) may also be used to call for continued vibration.

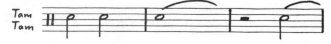

Write short stopped notes with eighth notes and staccato dots. Do not add words like *choke* or *sec.*

Indefinite pitch percussion instruments can play unmeasured tremolos, called *rolls*, and measured tremolos. Write out the first beat for a measured tremolo. A continuous roll over several measures is tied, and has an ending note if necessary.

Definite pitch instruments are capable of playing tremolos, trills, and tremolandos. Use the proper notation, as described in the previous chapter.

The tambourine may be shaken, as shown by the unmeasured tremolo, or played by rubbing the thumb across the head, as shown by the trill sign. Add the word *shake* or *thumb roll* to clarify the meaning of the sign.

Keyboard Instruments

Included in this section are the piano, organ, celesta, and harpsichord. The piano part for studio use is discussed in the section on guitar and rhythm instruments.

Staves and Braces. Write keyboard parts on two staff lines connected with a brace. Rule bars through both staves. Write the pedal part for the organ on a third staff line connected to the braced staves by a single line. Rule the bar lines separately through the braced staves and the pedal staff.

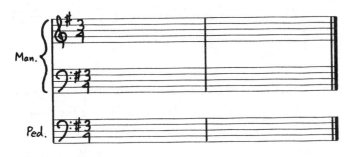

Alignment. Alignment of the notes is especially important in keyboard parts, as the notes must be aligned over two or three staves rather than just one. Often three or four voices occur simultaneously in the keyboard part; each part is complete in itself, with all the necessary rests aligned properly.

Beams. In addition to the normal use of beams in keyboard music, a beam may be used between the staves to carry a voice from one staff to another.

When writing a single voice across both staves, do not place rests in the unused space until the voice is exclusively in one staff again. If rests are included in the single voice, place them in the same staff as the note preceding them.

Arpeggios. All the notes of a chord are played at the same time unless an arpeggio sign is placed in front of the chord. The arpeggio will be played from bottom to top unless an arrow indicates otherwise. If the sign is broken, each hand will begin the arpeggio at the same time. Place the arpeggio sign before any accidentals.

Glissandos. Write glissandos for the keyboard as they are for any other instrument. The glissando is normally played on only the white keys.

Pedals (piano). The use of the pedals is usually left to the discretion of the player. If notating for the pedals is necessary, place brackets below the music. Most pedaling is done with the damper pedal, which holds the dampers away from the strings. Using the soft, or *una corda,* pedal is indicated by placing the term *U.C.* beneath the staff. The end of the passage is indicated by the term *T.C.* (*tre corde*). Using the sostenuto pedal is notated with brackets and the abbreviation *S.P.*

Slurs. To allow room for dynamic markings between staves, place slurs above the treble clef line and below the bass clef line, regardless of the stem direction.

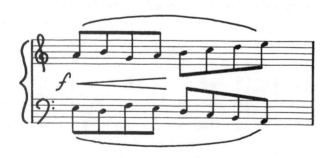

Staff Selection. The left hand will usually play the music on the lower staff and the right hand will play the upper staff. In some cases, however, the left hand may play so high or the right hand so low that it

is better to change the clef sign or to write for both hands on the same staff. The next example shows a passage written using three different methods. The first example is difficult to read because of the ledger lines. The second is an acceptable correction, and the third is easiest to read.

Sometimes it will be necessary for the left hand to play notes higher than the right hand. When this occurs, place the term *L.H.* at the beginning of the crossed hands.

An extra staff is sometimes added above or below a piano score to allow independent motion of another voice which would crowd the regular staves. Three independent voices may also be fit onto the same staff line if the alignment is offset slightly to make room for the stem.

Special Effects. The piano may be used for a variety of special sounds by striking the sounding board with the hand or other objects or by plucking the strings. Write any directions for an unusual effect above the staff and note them in the music with notes if pitches are produced, or use diamond and x-shaped notes and wavy lines if indefinite pitches are produced.

A common effect on the piano is sympathetic vibration. Several keys are silently depressed while other notes are played. The keys to be held down without playing are shown with diamond-shaped note heads.

Playing all the keys between two different pitches results in a tone cluster. Notate the tone cluster by drawing the upper and lower notes and connecting them with lines. If only white keys or black keys are to be played, a sharp sign or natural sign is placed above the tone cluster.

Registration (organ). Organs vary greatly in the available registration; it is usually best to leave the choice of registration to the player. Use only the more common stops to suggest a registration. Place the directions above the staff for the manuals, and above the pedal staff for the pedals. Indicate changes in registration as needed.

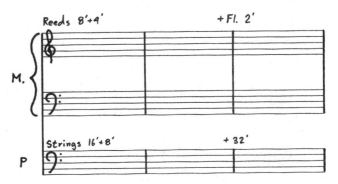

Harp

Harp parts are similar to piano parts, except that they usually contain more chords, arpeggios, and glissandos.

Pedals. The harp has seven strings per octave, one for each pitch. Each of the seven pitches, in all the octaves, is controlled by one of the seven pedals, allowing each pitch to be sharp, natural, or flat. The pedals can be set to allow the harp to play all of the notes in any one key, or the pedals can be set to produce enharmonic pitches, allowing all the strings to be tuned to as few as four different pitches.

Notate the settings for the pedals using a diagram of the pedals. The diagram shows the pedals in the order D-C-B-E-F-G-A. D, C, and B are controlled with the left foot, and E, F, G, and A are set with the right foot. Marks on the line show natural settings, marks above the line show flat settings, and marks below the line show sharp settings. The example shows how the pedals are set to play an E major scale.

Place the pedal diagram between the staves whenever it is needed. If only one or two pedals change at a particular point, show the change by simply listing the new pitch.

Allow enough time for the harpist to make pedal changes. One pedal may be changed with each foot almost instantaneously. The left foot may be used to change a right foot pedal, although this is very awkward. Two side-by-side pedals may be changed at the same time with one foot if the change is the same for both pedals, i.e. both changing from natural to sharp. Beyond moving a single pedal, allow about one beat of rest to move each additional pedal.

Chords. Write chords for the harp in the same manner as they are for the piano. Only four notes may be played simultaneously with each hand; the little finger is not used.

A chord will be rolled from bottom to top as it is played. Use an arpeggio sign for a more decided roll, and a bracket or the term *sec.* if no roll should occur.

Glissandos. Glissandos may be scales or chords. Write out a slow glissando; show a faster glissando with a wavy line or a straight line and the term *gliss*. A glissando should have a starting and ending note; a small stemless note is sometimes used. The following example shows arpeggios of the B-flat major scale and the dominant seventh chord. For the seventh chord, the pedals are set to enharmonics of the chord tones.

Harmonics. Natural harmonics on the harp sound one octave higher than written. Notate them by placing a circle above the notes.

Studio Music. Harp parts for studio use often leave the pedal settings and notes to the performer, giving only chord symbols and glissando markings. See the next section for the proper notation of chords.

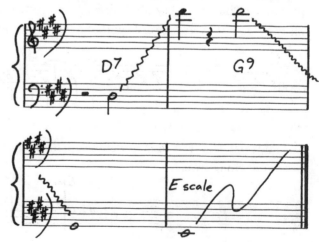

Guitar and Rhythm Instruments

This section discusses notation used in studio music for piano, guitar, trap set, and other rhythm instruments. The notation consists mostly of abbreviated notes and chord symbols. For more information on the preparation of studio music, see the section on planning studio parts in chapter 5.

Chord Symbols. Instead of writing out the notes of a chord, use a chord symbol with slash marks to show the rhythms. The following system of symbols is the most widely accepted, and the meaning of each symbol is clear.

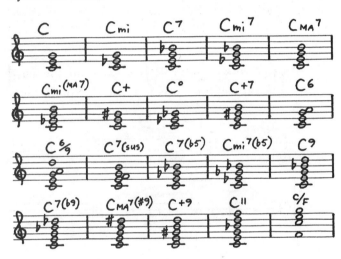

Rhythms. Use slash marks to indicate the rhythm. Straight quarter notes have no stems. Stem any deviation from straight quarter notes using traditional practices. Place chord symbols directly over the slash marks. Do not carry a chord symbol over a bar line.

If a particular note is to be on top, draw the top note and a long stem.

Guitar Parts. Guitar parts usually consist only of chords. For a melody, write line out with traditional notation. The guitar part is played one octave lower than written.

Bass guitars do not play chords. Write the part just as it would be for the string bass.

Piano Parts. The piano part will usually consist of a bass line for the left hand and chord symbols and slashes for the right hand. Write out particular chords and melodies as needed.

To indicate playing the bass line in octaves, place an *8* below the notes.

Trap Set Parts. The drum part is often very sketchy, telling the drummer when to play and what rhythm to use.

If more precise rhythms need to be shown, use the first space for the bass drum and the third space for the snare drum. Write cymbal parts in the fourth space with diamond and x-spaced note heads. Write other parts, such as wood blocks and cow bell, with regular notes in the fourth space. Write the name of the particular instrument above the staff. Write multiple pitch parts, such as the tom toms and temple blocks, with relative pitches in the third space, fourth space, and above the staff.

Vocal Music

The major difference between vocal music and any other instrument is the addition of text.

Clefs. Write four part vocal music on two or four lines joined with a bracket. On a two line part, sopranos and altos share the treble clef line, and tenors and basses share the bass clef line. On a four line part, each voice has its own line, with sopranos and altos in treble clef, tenors in treble clef but sung one octave lower, and basses in bass clef.

Beams and Flags. Write vocal music with beams and flags just like any other instrumental part. Do not use flags for every syllable or word. This only makes the music hard to read.

Slurs and Ties. Use slurs and ties in vocal music to mark the extension of words and syllables over several notes.

Text. Place the text for vocal music below the line of music. In a braced part, only one line of text is needed; place it between the lines of music. To make room for the text, place dynamics and other markings above the staff. If a divided part has a different text for each part, place the text for the upper part above the staff.

Use the text as it appears in the written source, with all the punctuation and capitalization of words retained, even if the sentence structure is distorted by the music.

Divide words into syllables as needed. Consult a dictionary if there is any question about the proper division of words.

Spacing and Alignment. Space the notes of the music to allow room for each word. The spacing of the notes may have to be wider than normal to accommodate longer words. In a melismatic passage, no additional space will be needed. Align the first letter of each syllable with its note.

Hyphens and Extension Lines. When a word is syllabified, place a hyphen between the syllables. Use only one hyphen, even if the syllables are widely spaced. If the end of a word extends over two or more notes, add an extension line. Place the extension line following any punctuation on the word.

Narration. Narration may be of three types: spoken parts without regard to rhythm or pitch, spoken parts with a specific rhythm, or spoken song, which shows rhythm and inflection but not actual pitches.

Place ordinary narration under an empty staff, spread out across the time span in which the narration is spoken.

For a specific rhythm, draw stems without notes to show the rhythm.

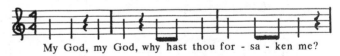

Write spoken song with notes showing relative pitches. Draw x-marks through the stems, and place the term *spoken* above the staff.

4. Preparing Scores

This chapter discusses the layout and preparation of scores for instrumental and vocal solos, duets, small ensembles, chamber groups, and large ensembles. Extracting individual parts from an ensemble score is discussed in the next chapter.

Page Layouts

For any first page layout center the title at the top of the page, place the name of the composer or arranger on the right, and, for a choral work, place the source of the text on the left. Place copyright information at the bottom of the page. The title and other information are needed only on the first page.

Connect the left side of all the staves in a score with a single bar line. Use a bracket to divide the instruments into choirs. Connect staves for identical instruments with an additional brace. Connect a double-line system for keyboard instruments or harp with a brace. Rule bar lines only through single choirs.

Piano, Celesta, Harpsichord, Harp. Write keyboard and harp parts on two staves joined with a bar line and braced together. Rule bar lines through both staves.

Piano, Four Hands. Music for piano duet is written in one of two ways. One method is to write the two parts out in a full score format, with the first part on top and the second part on the bottom. The second method, not used as frequently, places the sec-

ond part on the right-hand page and the first part on the left-hand page. Both parts must correspond measure for measure since each page turn serves both players. For either method, include all the necessary tempo and performance directions in both parts.

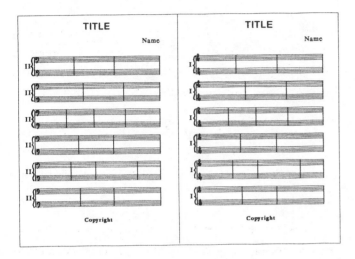

Organ. Write organ music on three staves, with the upper two staves connected with a brace. Rule bar lines separately through the manuals and pedals.

Organ and Piano. Place the organ below the piano in a score.

Solos with Piano Accompaniment. Write the solo part above the piano part. Special papers with

this particular ruling are available; they usually provide a little extra room between the piano staves and the solo staff. If the instrument playing the solo is a transposing instrument, the solo part on the score is often written in the same key as the piano part, and a separate part is extracted for the soloist.

Chamber Ensembles. Write music for chamber ensembles on as many staves as necessary, with the instruments bracketed into their individual choirs. See the section on orchestra scores for the proper order of the instruments. If the piano is included, place it at the bottom of the system. Write music for ensembles larger than an octet with the piano above the strings, as in a full score.

In most cases more than one score line of the music may be placed on a single page. If the system contains more than one choir, use double slash marks to separate the score lines.

trio:

duet:

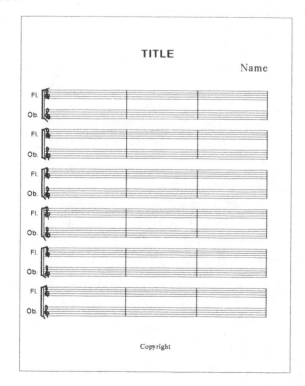

trio with piano:

quartet:

quintet:

quartet with piano:

sextet:

Percussion Ensemble. Percussion music differs from other instrumental music in that the players do not always play the same instrument throughout a piece. Because of this, each player has his own line of music, and changes in instruments are made on that line as the music progresses. In very complex music, where each player must play several different instruments, each instrument in a player's "percussion center" has its own line, and the lines are connected with a bracket for each player.

Write the score on blank staff paper, or hand-rule and duplicate a paper. If the paper is hand-ruled, use single lines for the indefinite pitch instruments.

Place the mallet instruments at the top of the score, followed by the indefinite pitch instruments from high to low pitch, followed by the tympani at the bottom of the score. If a keyboard instrument accompanies the ensemble, place the part below the tympani.

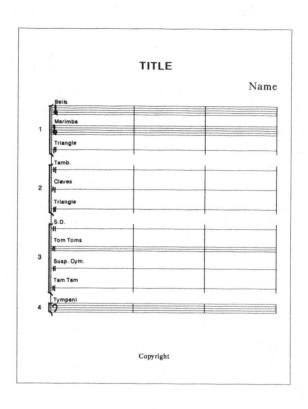

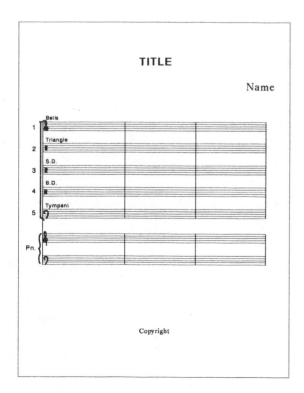

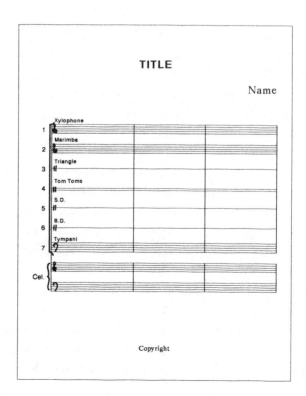

Orchestra. The following example shows, in the traditional order, most of the instruments that might be used in the orchestra. In most cases, many of the instruments listed in the example will not be used, and the lines may be removed from the format. Using pre-ruled papers will save considerable layout time if a suitable ruling can be found. An unused line may be deleted with correction tape, or simply left blank.

The example shows which instruments commonly share staves in the score. If there is considerable difference of rhythm between the parts, write the different parts on separate staves.

The piccolo often alternates with flute II, the English horn with oboe II, the bass clarinet with clarinet II, and the contrabassoon with bassoon II. If a player is to use an alternate instrument, note the instrument change as it occurs. A separate staff line is not needed for the alternate instrument.

If additional instruments are needed, add the extra lines in their proper place. Connect staves for identical instruments with a brace in addition to the choir bracket.

Theatre Orchestra, Studio Orchestra, Jazz Band. The theatre orchestra is used most often for musicals and contemporary Christian music. The layout is similar to that of a regular orchestra, but with the piano part placed at the bottom of the page. Also, instruments like saxophones, guitar, trap set, and voice are added to the score.

In professional situations woodwind parts may be combined, with players alternating between flute, oboe, clarinet, bass clarinet, alto saxophone, and tenor saxophone. A single player can usually play any three of the six instruments listed. Label the parts Woodwinds I and II, or label them Reeds I and II if only clarinet and saxophone will be played. Note the instrument to be played above the staff.

In a *church orchestration* extra parts for strings and less common instruments may be extracted for more common instruments. For instance, the viola

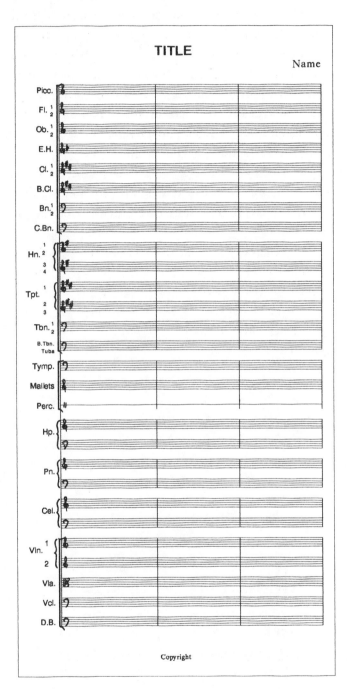

part may be written for the clarinet, the cello part for the bass clarinet, the horn part for the alto saxophone, and the bassoon part for the tenor saxophone. Also, more difficult parts written for professional players are often revised for the less advanced players in the typical church orchestra.

The studio orchestra is usually used for commercial music. It often has no vocal parts, and woodwind parts are more frequently combined.

The jazz band is used typically for playing dance music. The instrumentation is fairly standard, although saxophone players may alternate with clarinet or flute, and trumpets may alternate with the flügelhorn.

theatre orchestra:

studio orchestra:

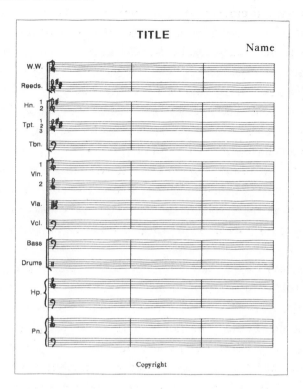

jazz band:

Symphonic Band. The symphonic band has a larger and more varied instrumentation than the orchestra. The following example shows nearly every instrument that might be used in the band, in its proper order. Many band works do not require English horn, E-flat clarinet, contrabass clarinet, harp, piano, and string bass. Consequently, some bands do not have access to these instruments. The alto clarinet is slowly being phased out as a common instrument; the part, if included, usually doubles the third clarinets or the bass clarinet. Add or delete lines as needed to fit a particular instrumentation. Using pre-ruled paper will save considerable layout time if a suitable ruling can be found.

Writing parts for both trumpets and cornets is optional. In transcriptions of orchestra works, the original trumpet parts are often retained from the orchestra version, and the cornets are an addition for the band. Both parts will usually be played on the trumpet rather than the cornet in the modern band.

Add additional parts such as a solo clarinet part, a solo trumpet part, or a flügelhorn part as needed.

Parts which usually share a staff, such as flutes, oboes, and trombones, may have separate staves if there is considerable rhythmic variation between the parts. Connect staves for identical instruments with a brace.

Instrumental Solos With Large Ensembles. Lay out a concerto or similar work with a solo instrument part accompanied by band or orchestra like the regular score, but with the solo part on its own line. In the orchestra, place the solo part just above the strings, and in the band, place it above the brass.

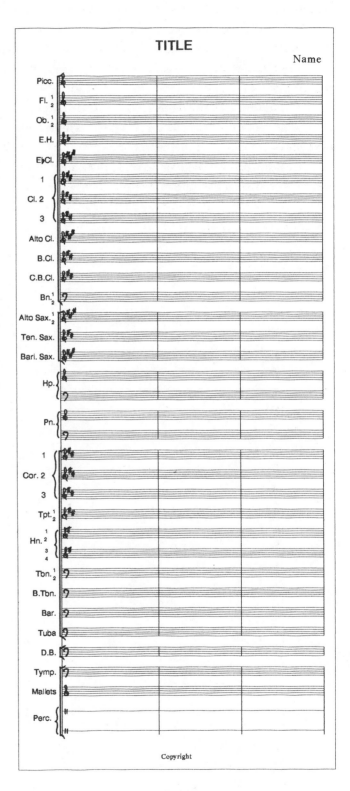

47

Vocal Music. Lay out vocal music in the same manner as instrumental music, with the exception that bar lines are ruled only through the single staff lines to avoid interfering with the text.

Choral music may be written on two staves, with one line of text between the staves if the motion in all voices is similar, or with each voice on its own line. If a work is to be performed *a cappella* (without accompaniment), reduce the parts to a piano part for rehearsal purposes. Add an extra staff as needed for a solo accompanied by the other voices.

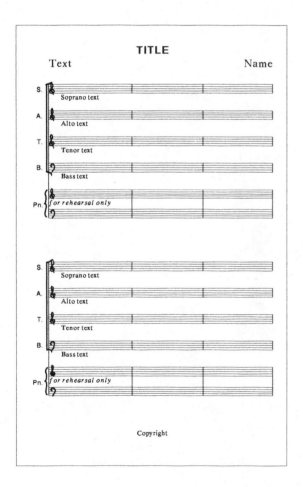

Condensed Scores

Condensed scores are used mostly for educational and studio music. Write the condensed score with three or four instrumental lines and a percussion line. Arrange the music by musical ideas, rather than by instrumental choirs; put the melody on the top line. Indicate the names of the instruments playing the different parts above the staff. Label changes in instrumentation at the point of change.

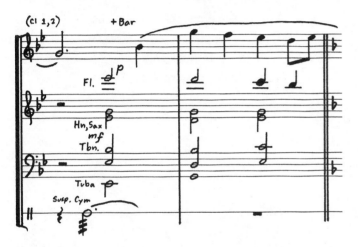

For studio music the condensed score is often called a cue sheet and is used by the conductor, technical coordinators, and tape editor. The score shows all the melodic and harmonic music, percussion, and vocal parts. Often the piano part with added cues may serve as a cue sheet.

For educational music most publishers prefer to issue a condensed score because it saves paper, while most conductors would rather have a full score so they can see every instrumental part clearly.

Rehearsal Numbers

Place the rehearsal numbers in a box both above and below the score line.

Key

Most scores are written with the parts of transposing instruments already transposed into the proper keys. Some arrangers, however, write all the parts in the same key; so they must be transposed when they are extracted. If this is the case, write the term *C-Score* in the upper left-hand side of the first page. Avoid using the C-Score when possible, especially in contemporary music where key signatures are not used on any of the parts.

Clef Signs and Meter Signatures

In rough drafts and sketches a clef sign is sometimes extended to cover several staves with a line extending downward from the bottom of the clef.

Each line usually has its own meter signature. If the meter changes frequently, using oversized meter signatures serving several lines of music can make meter changes easier to see.

Reducing Pages in a Full Score

Reduced scores are used most often in orchestra music. The first page of a full score must have all the parts listed, whether or not the instruments play on the first page. Following the first page, however, if only a few instruments play for several lines in the score, the resting parts may be left out and two or three lines of reduced score may be placed on one page. When the score is reduced, retain the order and choir division of the parts. Leave a blank line for extra space between each score line; the line may be covered with correction tape. Place double slash marks between the score lines at each side of the page.

Directions and Abbreviations

Label lines with the names of the instruments on each page of the score. If a part is being played *a2, solo,* or *with mutes,* place the term in parenthesis above the instrument's line at the beginning of each new score line following the initial statement of the term.

Place indications of tempo and changes in tempo above the top line, and restate them above the brass choir in a band and above the string choir in an orchestra. Place dynamics and style indications under each individual instrument line in the score.

Because space between lines in a score is lim-

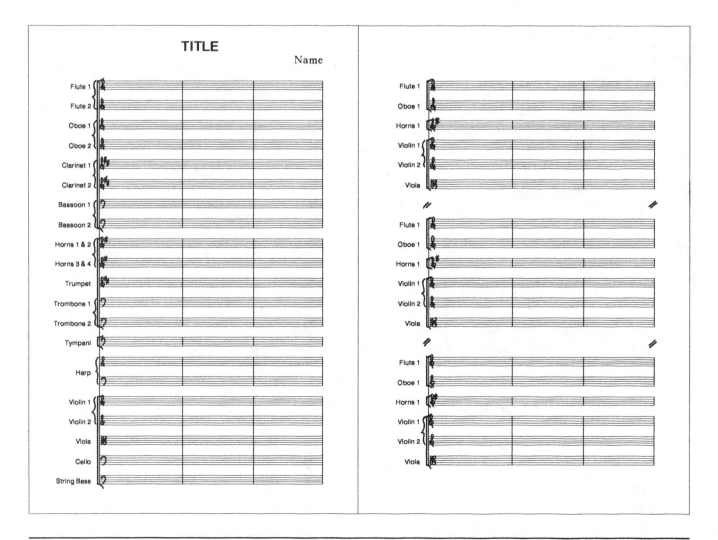

ited, the octave sign is used more frequently and stems are often made shorter than normal length. A very long slur can be drawn with the ruler as a straight line; curve the ends freehand after the body of the slur is drawn.

Full measures of rest in a score are often left blank rather than using a whole rest if the music will not be published.

An abbreviation found frequently in studio music is the term *Col* placed in the staff and followed by a thick wavy line. The term *Col* means "with the;" thus the term *Col flute* placed in a clarinet part means that the clarinet part is identical to the flute part. Indicate the proper transposition for the phrase with a small stemless note.

Cues

Write cues which are written into a part as a substitute for a missing instrument into the score, properly transposed and labeled. Cues which help a player make a proper entrance after a period of rest are not written in the score.

Spacing and Alignment

Spacing is not as critical in a score, because the score is often written using pre-ruled measures. Usually, a page has four measures, with an occasional deviation when there is a need to have more space for the music. Vertical alignment of the notes in the score is critical; sometimes good spacing is sacrificed to maintain alignment.

Samples of Actual Scores

On the following pages are samples of actual scores in manuscript for various instrumental and vocal arrangements. A great deal may be learned by studying these examples and other published music. Keep in mind when studying published music that many publishers make errors in notation.

NIGHT WILL COME AGAIN

Carl Sandburg

John Russell
1985

Used by permission.

From ''Meditation on a Psalm of David'' by Michael Mohn (the Baritone part for this piece is shown on page 65).

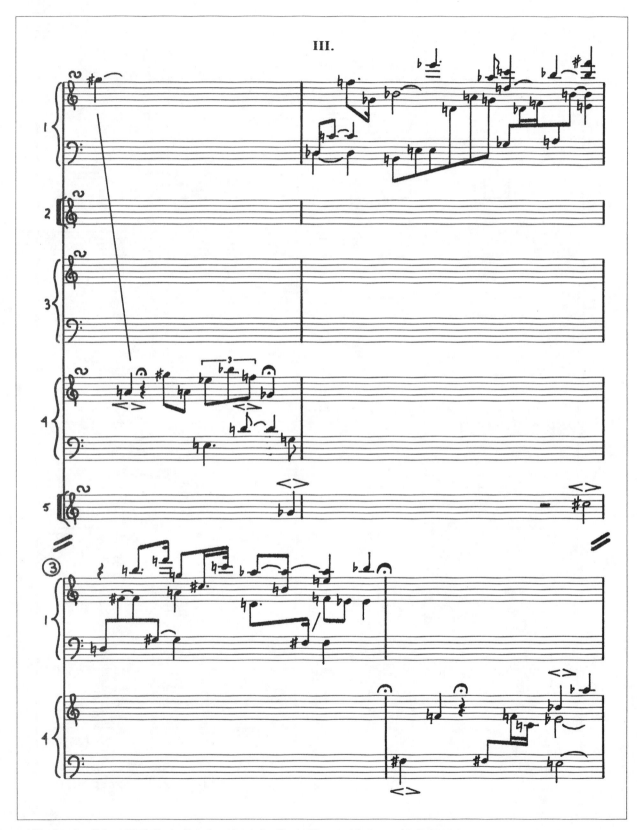

From "Endymion" for digital synthesizer by John Russell, used by permission.

From ''Endymion'' for digital synthesizer by John Russell, used by permission.

Clarinet Polka

Polish folk song

Traditional Polish folk song (extracted parts for this score appear on pages 68-71).

Traditional Polish folk song (extracted parts for this score appear on pages 68-71).

Traditional Polish folk song (extracted parts for this score appear on pages 68-71).

Traditional Polish folk song (extracted parts for this score appear on pages 68-71).

5. Extracting Parts

The individual parts from a full score must be extracted and written in a form that an individual player can read. Any instrumentalist can realize the need for a neat and accurate part to play from.

Layout

Write parts on blank staff papers. Paper with 10 staves is ideal for most copying. Single lines may be ruled on a blank sheet of paper for percussion parts.

On the first page center the title at the top, place the composer's name on the left, and place the name of the instrument on the right. Place copyright information at the bottom of the page. Extra room for the title may be obtained by blanking out the top line with correction tape. The title and other information are needed only on the first page.

Transposition

A copyist should be able to transpose parts easily and accurately; the skill is learned only with practice. Transposing parts is required when working with a C-score, when writing a score from an arranger's sketch, when writing parts where the *Col* abbreviation has been used, and when the arranger specifies that a section of music is to be copied into a different key.

Some unusual transpositions occur when the concert key contains four or more sharps:

- When transposing from the key of E:
  E-flat instruments play in the key of D-flat
  B-flat instruments play in the key of G-flat

- When transposing from the key of B:
  E-flat instruments play in the key of A-flat
  B-flat instruments play in the key of D-flat
  F instruments play in the key of G-flat

- When transposing from the key of C-sharp:
  E-flat instruments play in the key of B-flat
  B-flat instruments play in the key of E-flat
  F instruments play in the key of A-flat

In orchestra work when the concert key has five or more sharps, the A-clarinet and C-trumpet are often used instead of the B-flat instruments.

Editing

When extracting parts, do not simply copy the score, taking for granted that the composer or arranger has not made any mistakes. Instead, watch carefully for incorrect notation, missing rests, wrong transposition, missing directions, and unclear notation. Correct any problems in the score as well as in the part. Usually the composer's intent can be determined by studying the other rhythms and harmony in the score; if there is any question, discuss the problem with the composer.

Arrangers often use many abbreviations, such as the octave sign and the half measure repeat. Write the music out properly for the player.

If the clef changes in the middle of a passage, the change might be more clear if the clef is changed earlier in the passage.

Chromatic passages are most clearly written if sharps are used on ascending passages and flats on descending passages. Using enharmonic equivalents may make a passage easier to read.

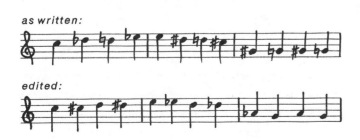

Rehearsal Numbers

Include every rehearsal number in the extracted part. Break up a multiple bar rest to show the location of the rehearsal numbers, key and meter changes, and tempo changes, if necessary. If actual measure numbers are used for the rehearsal numbers, missing measures in a part are easier to see.

Page Turns

Page turns are one of the biggest problems to deal with when extracting parts. If the part will fit onto one or two pages, a turn is not necessary. When the part is longer than two pages, plan the part so the page turn occurs during a period of rest. Make the measures a little shorter in order to reach a rest by the end of the page, or leave blank lines so the page can be turned at an earlier rest period. If a turn can not be made during a period of rest, half the instrumental section will be forced to drop out to turn the page while the other half plays, unless the notes can be played with one hand. When a page turn must be made very quickly or when the turn is in a bad location, place the term *V.S. (Volti Subito)* under the last measure of the page.

Page turns in a piano solo part are not a problem, as a person is often present to turn the pages. An ensemble piano part, however, should have planned page turns.

Page Numbers

The first page of a work is usually a right-hand page and is not numbered. Pages following the first are numbered consecutively, even numbered pages on the left and odd numbered pages on the right; thus page turns will occur on the odd numbered pages. In the case of a two-page part, the first page, which is on the left, is numbered page 2; page 1 is the outside cover.

Pages may be numbered in the upper center, lower center, or upper corner. The corner location has the advantage of insuring correct duplication, since reversing a page would place the number on the inside corner.

Spacing

While extracting a part, look ahead in the score to make sure there is enough room in the line for all the upcoming music. Copyists sometimes run out of space for a long measure because they do not look ahead and space properly at the beginning. Cramming notes into the end of the line or leaving blank space at the end of the line are both signs of amateur work.

poor:

poor:

correct:

Measures should be of the proper size to fit the music which they contain. Rule out equal-sized measures only if each measure contains the same number of notes.

Planning Educational Music

Copying parts for educational use requires careful planning, because publishers insist that the music fill all the pages, with the double bar at the end of the line at the bottom of the last page. This tradition is apparently based on the idea that if people see half a page blank, they feel they are not getting their money's worth.

The length of the part may be adjusted by spreading the measures out or cramming them together. Also, papers with varying numbers of lines may be used, and one or more lines may be deleted from the top of the part to allow for larger lettering in the title.

When planning the part, it is helpful to draw out a chart of the part. Assume that the part will have 10 staves per page, six small measures or three large measures per line, and two blank staves for the title. Begin checking off measures in the chart, and use a number to show multiple bar rests. Also include rehearsal locations on the chart. A complete chart might appear like the following example.

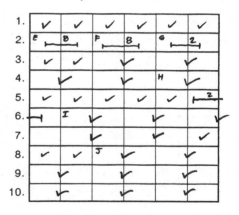

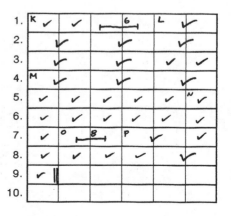

After the chart is constructed, adjust the page layout by varying the number of measures per line and the length of multiple bar rests. Note that the page must be turned at the end of page 1, but not after page 2. The adjusted part may appear as follows.

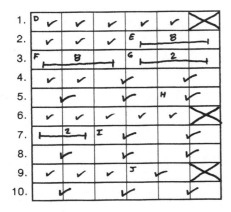

The publisher will usually typeset the title and copyright information. Pencil the title in lightly so it can be erased later.

Planning Studio Music

Just the opposite of educational music, studio music is written with the phrasing of the music and ease of reading in mind, with little regard for the length of the part.

Most popular music is written in eight measure phrases, which naturally divide into four measure halves and two measure quarters. The music can be made easier to read by writing four measures per line to retain the natural balance of the phrases.

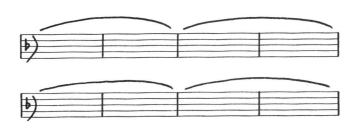

If an odd phrase is written, regain the balance of the part by writing a three measure or five measure line. Longer or shorter multiple bar rests can also be used to regain balance of the phrases.

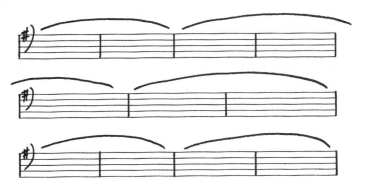

On a balanced part write an odd numbered multiple bar rest in the space of one measure and an even numbered rest in the space of two measures.

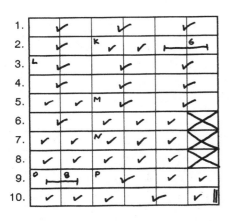

Place repeat signs, *Dal Segno* signs, and second endings at the beginning of the line. Some three measure lines may be needed to regain balance of the part.

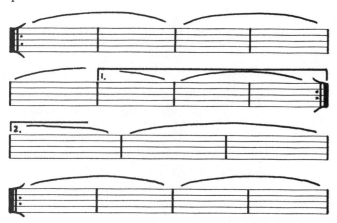

On studio music box words placed above the staff and underline words placed below the staff.

Samples of Actual Parts

On the following pages are samples of actual parts for instrumental music. A great deal may be learned by studying these examples and other published examples. Keep in mind that publishers often make mistakes in published parts.

Meditation on a Psalm of David

Michael Mohn

Clarinet Polka

Polish folk song

Clarinet Polka

Polish folk song

6. Proofreading, Duplicating, and Binding

Proofreading

Proofread scores and parts carefully for accuracy. The most common errors will be incorrect transposition, missing accidentals, and missing beams and flags.

To proofread a part against the score, check the part for key and time signatures, tempo markings, and dynamic markings. Next, check for rehearsal numbers; then count all the measures between the numbers to make sure a measure is not missing. Then, check every note and rest in the part with the score. Do this with one finger on the part and one finger on the score, checking it one measure at a time. This is a tedious process, but it will usually reveal nearly all the mistakes. After checking the parts visually, play through each part on the piano. As the part is played, pay special attention to missing beams, flags, and rests by counting the beats in each measure.

Make proofreading marks on a master for photoengraving very lightly with a hard blue pencil. For vocal text use standard proofreader's symbols. Note a correction at the mistake and also in the margin. When correcting notes, draw a small portion of staff to show the correction.

Duplicating

Most publishing houses photoengrave music from autographs. If a work is to be photoengraved, prepare the autograph on white paper using heavy ink.

A few smaller publishers use the diazo process, which is similar to the blueprinting process used by draftsman. The diazo process has the advantage that large, odd size scores may be duplicated inexpensively. On the other hand, the master must be prepared on vellum, which is not as convenient as plain paper.

The majority of unpublished work is reproduced by xerographic copying on ordinary office equipment. Prepare masters for copying on 11 by 17 inch, 8 1/2 by 11 inch, and 8 1/2 by 14 inch papers. Even if no extra copies of a part are needed, duplicate the part anyway so a backup copy is available if the part is lost.

When using xerographic equipment, the music may be printed on both sides of the paper, minimizing the bulk of the part. If the pages have been numbered correctly, odd numbered pages will always be on the right and even numbered pages will be on the left.

Binding Parts

Parts written on 8 1/2 by 11 inch paper can be duplicated onto 11 by 17 inch paper which is then folded in half; thus no binding is necessary. Up to three sheets of 11 by 17 inch paper may be folded together without any binding. Saddle staple parts containing more than three sheets.

If the part has too many pages to be folded, a good but slightly expensive alternative is a plastic spiral binding. Print the music on both sides of 8 1/2 by 11 inch sheets of paper.

Never staple a part through the margin, because it will not lie flat on the music stand.

Parts printed on one side of the paper may be bound by accordion folding the parts. White masking tape is better than plastic tape for binding, because it does not wear out and crack. Tape the pages together on the back side in a continuous strip, and fold the part into an accordion. Paste the pages together at the hinge side with a dab of a glue stick to keep the accordion together. Complete the binding with a strip of tape on the outside spine to make the part into a book.

Binding Scores

Scores are usually larger then individual parts and are often written on 11 by 17 inch paper. The score may be photoreduced to 8 1/2 by 11 inch paper and bound by folding and saddle stapling, as many large publishing houses do, but this makes the print so small that it is difficult to read. A better alternative is to copy the score onto both sides of 11 by 17 inch paper and bind it with a plastic spiral binding. Scores may also be bound with an accordion fold and masking tape.

Appendix A
Instrumentation

This appendix provides information about the ranges, availability, and capabilities of the various instruments used in musical performance. Only traditional instruments are discussed; information about digital electronic instruments is beyond the scope of this book.

1. Traditional Ensembles

Piano, Four Hands

The term *Piano, four hands* indicates that two people will play the same instrument, one person playing the high notes and the other playing the low notes. The term *piano duet* applies to a work played on two pianos.

Piano Trio

A piano trio consists of violin, cello, and piano. The viola may be added to form a piano quartet.

String Quartet

The string quartet is composed of first and second violin, viola, and cello.

Woodwind Quintet

The woodwind quintet consists of flute, oboe, clarinet, horn, and bassoon. The horn, although not a woodwind, blends well with the woodwinds and fills in the mid-range between the bassoon and clarinet.

Saxophone Quartet

The saxophone quartet is composed of soprano saxophone, alto saxophone, tenor saxophone, and baritone saxophone. The bass saxophone, a rarely seen instrument, may be added to form a saxophone quintet.

Brass Quintet

The brass quintet usually consists of first and second trumpet, horn, trombone, and tuba.

Brass Band

The brass band is common in Europe, and is slowly gaining popularity in America. The traditional instrumentation of the brass band is as follows:

E-flat Cornet
Cornets 1, 2, 3, and 4
Flügelhorn
Tenor or French Horns 1, 2, and 3
Baritone Horns
Euphoniums
Trombones 1 and 2
Bass Trombone
E-flat Tubas
B-flat Tubas

Orchestra

By far the largest volume of music literature is written for the orchestra. The core of the orchestra consists of the strings; a typical string orchestra might have 14 first violins, 12 second violins, 10 violas, 8 cellos, and 6 basses.

The Baroque orchestra, in addition to the strings, will have a harpsichord or pipe organ, and may have parts for one or more of the following instruments:

Recorders 1 and 2
Flutes 1 and 2
Oboes 1 and 2
Bassoons 1 and 2
Cornets 1, 2, and 3
Trumpets 1 and 2
Horns 1 and 2
Trombones 1 and 2
Tympani

The symphony orchestra, in addition to the strings, may add any of the following instruments:

Piccolo
Flutes 1 and 2
Oboes 1 and 2
English Horn
Clarinets 1 and 2
Bass Clarinet
Bassoons 1 and 2

Contrabassoon
Horns 1, 2, 3, and 4
Trumpets 1 and 2
Trombones 1, 2, and 3
Tuba
Tympani
Percussion
Harp
Piano
Organ
Celesta

In smaller orchestras the piccolo often alternates with flute 2, the English horn with oboe 2, the bass clarinet with clarinet 2, and the contrabassoon with bassoon 2. The amateur orchestra often has no English horn, contrabassoon, harp, or celesta. Writing important parts for oboe and bassoon into other instrument parts using cue notes is wise, as these instruments are not as common.

Studio Orchestra

A typical studio orchestra has 4 first violins, 4 second violins, 3 violas, and 2 cellos. The electric bass guitar is often used instead of the string bass. The following parts are usually used in addition to the strings:

Woodwinds 1, 2, and 3   (flute, oboe, clarinet,
          bass clarinet, alto saxophone, tenor
          saxophone)
Horns 1 and 2
Trumpets 1, 2, and 3
Trombones 1 and 2
Tuba
Tympani
Trap Set
Percussion
Piano
Organ
Harp
Electric Guitar

The woodwind players can usually play any three of the six instruments listed during a studio work. Separate parts for each woodwind instrument are usually written for the amateur church orchestra. Also,

because many churches lack enough string players, a clarinet part is usually written to cover the viola part, and a bass clarinet part is written to cover the cello part. Flute players can play the violin parts directly.

Band

The major difference between the symphony orchestra and the modern symphonic band is the lack of string instruments. The addition of saxophones and baritones, as well as the larger clarinet and trumpet sections, takes the place of the string parts.

A typical symphonic band may have the following instrumentation:

Piccolo
Flutes 1 and 2
Oboes 1 and 2
English Horn
E-flat Clarinet
Clarinets 1, 2, and 3
(alto clarinet)
Bass Clarinets
Contrabass Clarinet
Bassoons 1 and 2
Alto Saxophones 1 and 2
Tenor Saxophones
Baritone Saxophone
Cornets 1, 2, and 3
Trumpets 1 and 2
Horns 1, 2, 3, and 4
Trombones 1 and 2
Bass Trombones
Baritones or Euphoniums
Tubas
String Bass
Harp
Piano
Tympani
Percussion

Amateur bands often have no oboes, English horn, bassoons, E-flat clarinet, contrabass clarinet, string bass, or harp. Writing cues for these instruments into other parts is wise. Unlike the orchestra, where wind parts are added only as needed for each particular work, all the instruments in the band are usually used, except for the piccolo, English horn, E-flat clarinet, and contrabass clarinet. These players usually alternate with a more frequently used instrument. String bass, harp, piano, and percussion may be used as needed, just as in the orchestra.

The alto clarinet is not used very often as a band instrument; the alto clarinet part will usually duplicate the third clarinet or bass clarinet part. The contra-alto clarinet may be used instead of the contrabass clarinet, if desired.

Separate cornet and trumpet parts are optional; frequently only three trumpet parts are used. In either case, all the parts are usually played on the trumpet. The flügelhorn may be added as needed; it will be played by one of the trumpet players.

Marching Band

The marching band, usually seen at football games and in parades, uses an instrumentation similar to the symphonic band; the major difference is in the percussion section. The size of the marching band may be as large as 100 to 150 instruments, with 20 to 30 percussion instruments which have been designed to be carried. Some marching bands also have instruments which cannot be carried, such as electric bass guitar, electronic keyboard, tympani, trap set, and other large percussion instruments. These instruments are usually played from the sidelines of the football field while the band marches on the field.

The typical marching band has the following parts:

Flutes
Clarinets
Alto Saxophones 1 and 2
Tenor Saxophones
Baritone Saxophones
Trumpets 1, 2, and 3
Horns
Trombones 1 and 2
Bass Trombones
Baritones and Tubas
Snare Drums
Tom Toms (3 to 5 different pitches per player)
Timbales (a Latin instrument, similar to tom toms)
Bass Drums (2 to 4 different pitches)
Crash Cymbals (2 to 4 different pitches)
Orchestra Bells
Marimba
Xylophone
Tympani (occasionally)
Bass Guitar (occasionally)

2. Instrument Names, Abbreviations, and Ranges

The instruments listed on the following pages, with the exception of the contrabassoon, bass saxophone, and celesta, are usually available to most professional and semi-professional instrumentalists.

Instruments which do not have a range given in the amateur category are usually not available to amateur musicans. The ranges given for voice are often exceeded in solo work.

Woodwinds

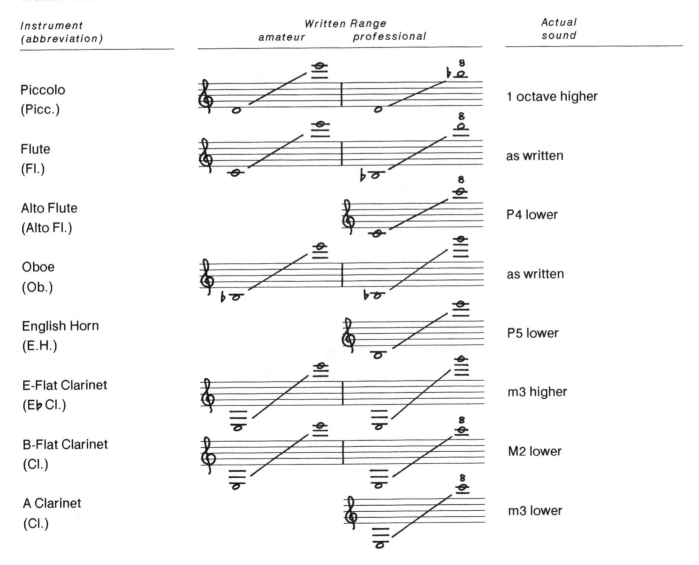

Instrument (abbreviation)	Written Range — amateur — professional	Actual sound
Piccolo (Picc.)		1 octave higher
Flute (Fl.)		as written
Alto Flute (Alto Fl.)		P4 lower
Oboe (Ob.)		as written
English Horn (E.H.)		P5 lower
E-Flat Clarinet (E♭ Cl.)		m3 higher
B-Flat Clarinet (Cl.)		M2 lower
A Clarinet (Cl.)		m3 lower

Instrument (abbreviation)	Written Range amateur / professional	Actual sound
Alto Clarinet (Alto Cl.)		M6 lower
Bass Clarinet (B. Cl.)		1 octave & M2 lower
Contra-alto Clarinet (C.Al. Cl.)		1 octave & M6 lower
Contrabass Clarinet (C.B. Cl.)		2 octaves & M2 lower
Bassoon (Bn.)		as written
Contrabassoon (C. Bn.)		1 octave lower
Soprano Saxophone (Sop. Sax.)		M2 lower
Alto Saxophone (Alto Sax.)		M6 lower
Tenor Saxophone (Ten. Sax.)		1octave & M2 lower
Baritone Saxophone (Bari. Sax.)		1 octave & M6 lower
Bass Saxophone (Bass Sax.)		2 octaves & M2 lower

Brass

Instrument (abbreviation)	Written Range		Actual sound
	amateur	professional	

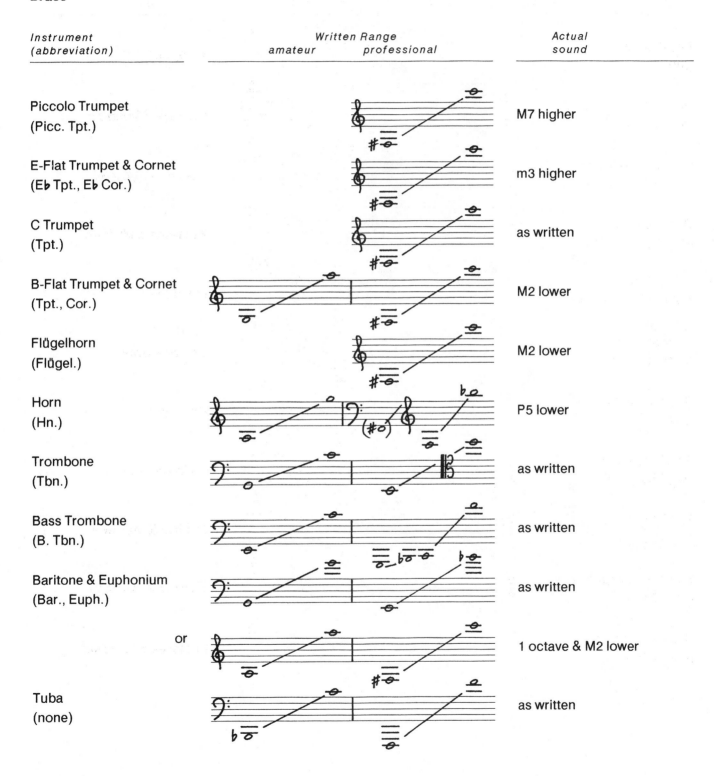

Piccolo Trumpet (Picc. Tpt.) — M7 higher

E-Flat Trumpet & Cornet (E♭ Tpt., E♭ Cor.) — m3 higher

C Trumpet (Tpt.) — as written

B-Flat Trumpet & Cornet (Tpt., Cor.) — M2 lower

Flügelhorn (Flügel.) — M2 lower

Horn (Hn.) — P5 lower

Trombone (Tbn.) — as written

Bass Trombone (B. Tbn.) — as written

Baritone & Euphonium (Bar., Euph.) — as written

or — 1 octave & M2 lower

Tuba (none) — as written

Percussion (definite pitch)

Instrument (abbreviation)	Written Range		Actual sound
	amateur	professional	

Tympani (Tymp.)		as written
Chimes (none)		as written
Xylophone (Xylo.)		1 octave higher
Marimba (Mar.)		as written
Vibraphone (Vibes.)		as written
Bells (none)		2 octaves higher

Percussion (indefinite pitch)

Name	Abbreviation	Name	Abbreviation
Snare Drum	S.D.	Tambourine	Tamb.
Tom Toms	Toms.	Triangle	Trgl.
Bass Drum	B.D.	Castanets	Casts.
Cymbals (Crash)	Cym.	Bongos	Bong.
Suspended Cymbal	Susp. Cym.	Claves	none
Antique Cymbals	Ant. Cym.	Güiro	none
High Hat Cymbals	Hi.Hat.	Maracas	none
Gong	none	Temple Blocks	Temp. Bl.
Tam Tam	none	Wood Blocks	Wd. Bl.

(Spell out the names of any other percussion instruments)

Strings

Instrument (abbreviation)	Written Range amateur professional	Actual sound
Violin (Vln.)		as written
Viola (Vla.)		as written
Cello (Vcl.)		as written
String Bass (D.B.)		1 octave lower
Guitar (none)		1 octave lower
Bass Guitar (none)		1 octave lower

Recorders (Baroque)

Instrument	Written Range	Actual sound
Sopranino Recorder (Sopranino Rec.)		1 octave higher
Soprano Recorder (Sop. Rec.)		1 octave higher
Alto Recorder (Alto Rec.)		as written
Tenor Recorder (Ten. Rec.)		as written
Bass Recorder (Bass Rec.)		as written

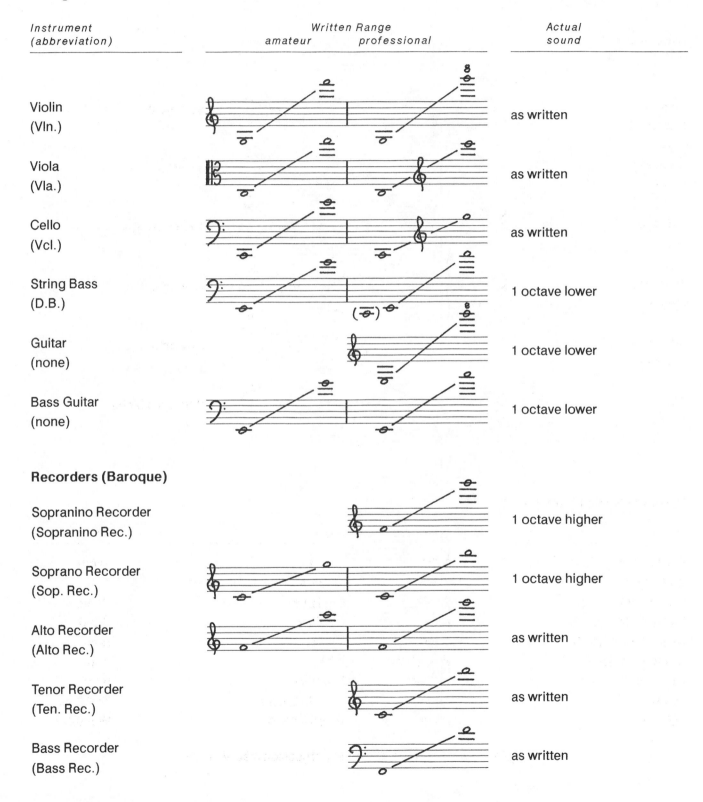

Keyboard Instruments

Instrument (abbreviation)	Written Range	Actual sound
Piano (Pn.)		as written
Organ (Org.)		as written (8')
		as written (8')
Harpsichord (Hpscd.)		as written (8')
Celesta (Cel.)		1 octave higher
Harp (Hp.)		as written

Voice

Instrument (abbreviation)	Written Range amateur professional	Actual sound
Soprano (S.)		as written
Alto (A.)		as written
Tenor (T.)		as written
or		1 octave lower
Baritone (Bar.)		as written
Bass (B.)		as written
Children		

3. Relative Sounding Ranges of the Instruments

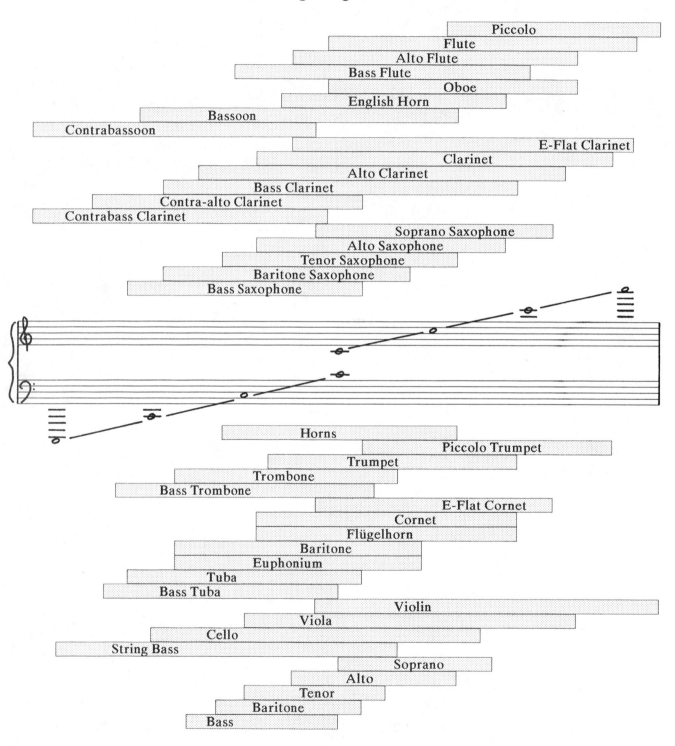

4. Basic Principles of Sound Production

Sound

Musical notes are created by the vibration of air at a controlled rate. Different pitches are perceived when the air vibrates at different frequencies; the human ear can hear frequencies from 16 cycles per second to greater than 16,000 cycles per second.

Musical instruments produce sounds by setting air into motion with a vibrating string as in the violins, a vibrating reed as in the woodwinds, vibrating lips as in the brass, a vibrating surface as in the percussion, or vibrating vocal chords when a person sings.

The Harmonic Series

The harmonic series is most easily understood by looking at a plucked string. The string vibrates with a node (a point of no movement) at each end, producing a pitch called the *fundamental* which is determined by the length and tension of the string. The string can also vibrate in halves, with a node in the center, producing a higher pitch of twice the fundamental frequency called the *second partial*. Similarly, the string can vibrate in thirds, to produce the *third partial*, fourths, to produce the *fourth partial*, and so on.

The harmonic series continues indefinitely, with the frequency increasing by multiples of the fundamental frequency. The harmonic series applies not only to strings, but to any vibrating object or to air vibrating in a tube. The actual vibration of the string is very complex; the diagrams below are simplified to show the locations of the nodes.

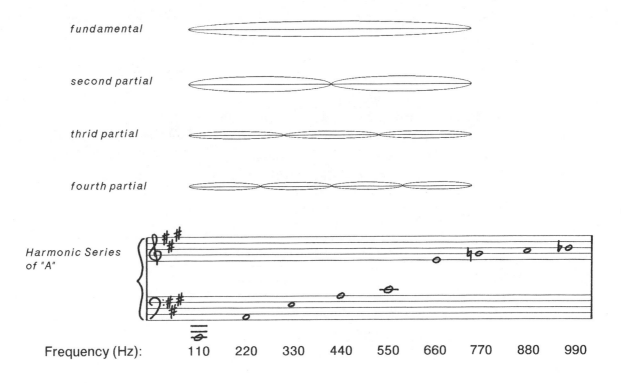

The *timbre*, or characteristic sound of an instrument, is determined by the intensity of each partial, or *overtone*, that sounds at the same time as the fundamental, as well as the unstable sound which the instrument produces at the beginning and end of notes. The particular overtones heard on an instrument are affected by the way in which the air is vibrated and, in wind instruments, by the shape of the tube in which the air vibrates. Bends in the tubing have no effect on the sound; they simply make the instrument easier to handle.

String Instruments

When a string is plucked or bowed, it vibrates at a frequency based on its length, diameter, and tension. One end of the string is held by the bridge, which transfers the vibration of the string to the hollow body of the instrument, which, in turn, vibrates the air. Electronic pickups, such as those found on electric pianos and guitars, may also be used to electronically transfer the vibration of the string to an amplifier. Different pitches are produced on a string when its effective length is made shorter by pinching it against the fingerboard.

Woodwind Instruments

A woodwind instrument is a tube open at one end and closed at the other, with a method of setting the air in motion at the closed end, either with a vibrating cane reed or with a blow-hole. Holes drilled down the length of the tube can be opened or closed one at a time to change the effective length of the tube. The fundamental for each effective tube length is played unless the player *overblows* the instrument, causing the second or third partial to be produced.

The shape of the tube, either cylindrical or conical, and the method of vibrating the air, either with a blow-hole, single reed, or double reed, determines the timbre of the instrument.

Brass

The brass are acoustically similar to the woodwinds except that the air is vibrated by buzzing the lips into a mouthpiece at one end of the tube. The tube has a very small diameter in relation to its length, making it easy to overblow by tightening the lips. This allows the player to pick out almost any of the partials on a given length of tube.

To play the notes which lie between the partials of the open tube, the player changes the length of the tube to produce a lower fundamental pitch and a different harmonic series. This is accomplished by extending a movable slide, as on the trombone, or by opening one or more valves which divert the air into additional loops of tubing.

The timbre of the instrument is dependent on the shape of the tubing, either cylindrical or conical, and on the shape of the mouthpiece, either funnel shaped or cup shaped.

Percussion Instruments

Percussion instruments vibrate the air with a membrane or a metal surface, which is usually struck with a stick, hammer, mallet, or the hands.

5. Guide to the Common Instruments

Flutes

The flute family is composed of cylindrical wood-wind instruments which produce sound when air is blown across a hole at one end of the tube. The tube has holes which are opened and closed to change the effective length of the tube.

The modern flute, which is usually made of metal and has a complex key system, evolved from a Baroque instrument called the *transverse flute*, which was simply a wooden tube with six finger holes and a blow-hole drilled in it.

The flute can be found in four sizes: the piccolo, the (soprano) flute, the alto flute, and the bass flute. The bass flute is four feet long, bent back on itself so the player can reach the blow-hole; it plays so softly that it is almost always amplified electronically during performance. The piccolo and flute are common instruments, the alto flute is usually available at the professional level, and the bass flute is relatively rare.

The flute produces a pure sound, almost a perfect sine wave. Flute players will normally play with a vibrato to add some color and depth to the tone. The timbre of the flute varies considerably from the low flutes to the high flutes and from the low range to the high range of each flute. The lower notes are warm and full, while the higher notes are more shrill. The dynamic compass of the flute also varies with the pitch; low notes cannot be played loudly, and high notes cannot be played softly.

The flute is an agile instrument. Single notes may be played quickly, using a technique called *double tonguing*, and notes are easily slurred across large intervals. In the lowest range of the soprano flute and on the alto and bass flute short staccato notes are impossible to play.

The recorder, a close relative to the flute, is the only Baroque wind instrument which is commonly seen today. Instead of blowing across a blow-hole, the

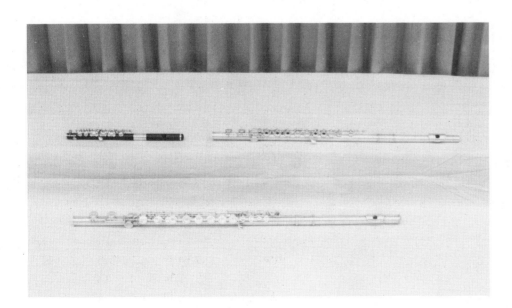

Flutes:
(small to large) piccolo,
(soprano) flute,
alto flute.

player blows into the end, and the air stream is then directed across a wooden lip to produce the sound. The recorder can be found in five common sizes: the sopranino recorder, the soprano recorder, the alto recorder, the tenor recorder, and the bass recorder. The sopranino, soprano, and alto recorders are the most common recorders made; the tenor and bass are usually available at the professional level. The different sizes of recorders are pitched in different keys; but the player transposes the music as he plays, rather than playing from a transposed part for a particular size recorder. This gives the individual player the choice of which recorder to play for a particular passage.

The recorder plays softly, and there is little control over the dynamics; the notes get louder as they ascend in pitch. Any dynamic markings in recorder music will generally be ignored. Because the recorder has no key mechanism, chromatic passages are difficult to play because the accidentals require awkward fingerings.

Double Reeds

The oboe and bassoon are conical shaped instruments which produce sound with double reeds made of cane. Although the instruments are not related, they are often grouped together because of their double reeds. The oboe is an old instrument, a descendant of the Renaissance instrument called the *shawm*. By the time of the Baroque the oboe was a standard instrument, and it has not changed much except for the evolution of its key system.

Oboes are available in two sizes, one called the oboe, and the other called the English horn. "English horn" is a misnomer, as the instrument is neither English nor a horn. The English horn differs from the oboe in that it has a bulb at the end, called the *liebesfuss*, which darkens the tone of the lowest notes. The oboe is common, and the English horn is usually available at the professional level.

Oboes are usually played with a vibrato. The tone is reedy and nasal sounding. The lowest notes are difficult to play softly and have a honking sound. As the pitch rises to the extreme range, the sound becomes thin and piercing, even if played softly.

The bassoon is also an old instrument, a descendent of the *curtail*. The modern bassoon has a surprisingly primitive fingering system; any attempt to modernize the fingering system destroys its characteristic sound.

Double Reeds:
(small to large) oboe, English horn, bassoon.

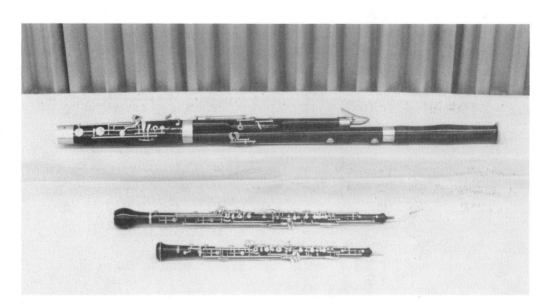

The bassoon family contains two instruments, the bassoon and the contrabassoon. The bassoon is an eight-foot long tube which folds back on itself once. The contrabassoon is twice as long, folds back on itself four times, and plays one octave lower than the bassoon. The bassoon is fairly common; the contrabassoon is relatively rare, even at the professional level.

The sound of the bassoon is reedy and nasal, but somewhat darker than the oboe. The dynamic compass of the instrument is slightly limited; the lower notes are difficult to play softly. The contrabassoon, because of its length, is a sluggish instrument; short staccato passages are impossible to play on the contrabassoon. *Multiphonics*, or the production of several pitches at the same time, can be produced on almost any instrument, but they are easiest to produce on the bassoon.

Clarinets

Clarinets are cylindrical woodwind instruments with a single reed. The clarinets are the largest family of woodwind instruments, and they are the most common of all the instruments.

The clarinet is a modern instrument; it became popular during the life of Mozart, who wrote a large amount of music for the basset horn, the closest ancestor of the clarinet; near the end of his life, Mozart also wrote for the clarinet.

The clarinet is available in seven sizes: the E-flat clarinet, B-flat clarinet, A clarinet, alto clarinet, bass clarinet, contra-alto clarinet, and contrabass clarinet.

The E-flat clarinet is common at the professional level and is usually found in the band. It has a bright, almost shrill, tone and is agile throughout its range.

The B-flat clarinet is the most common clarinet. It has a bright, hollow sound, which is warm and rich in the low range and trumpet-like in the upper range. The A clarinet is designed to play music in sharp keys. Although the A clarinet is not called for in most modern music, most professional clarinetists own one because it is frequently used in eighteenth and nineteenth century music. Its tone is nearly the same as the B-flat clarinet.

The alto clarinet is usually found only in the band, where it is slowly being phased out as a common instrument due to its undeserved bad reputation. It earned this reputation because band directors usually gave it to the less skilled players. The composers,

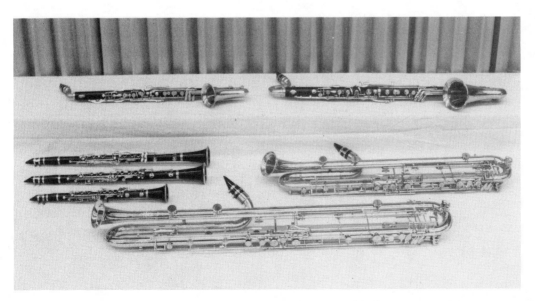

Clarinets:
(clockwise, from left)
E-flat (soprano) clarinet,
B-flat (soprano) clarinet,
A (soprano) clarinet,
alto clarinet,
bass clarinet,
contra-alto clarinet,
contrabass clarinet.

seeing this trend, began to write easier parts doubled by other instruments, which encouraged the directors to continue giving the instrument to the less skilled players. In the hands of a good clarinetist, the alto clarinet is one of the most versatile of all the clarinets. It has the largest range of all the wind instruments.

The bass clarinet is fairly common and adds a rich warm tone to the clarinet choir. Like the alto clarinet it has an extensive range; but, unfortunately, it is often given to the less skilled players in the band. The instrument has a curved neck and bell to make it easier to handle.

The contra-alto and contrabass clarinets are the lowest and richest sounding of all the clarinets. The contrabass clarinet has the same range as the contrabassoon, but it has the advantage of being much more agile. The lowest notes of the contrabass clarinet are so rich in harmonics that the fundamental cannot be recognized unless another instrument plays the fundamental pitch in a higher octave. Because the contra-alto and contrabass clarinets are usually played in the lowest range, they do not have the proper key system to play in the extreme high range.

The clarinet, unlike most of the other instruments, is normally played without vibrato. The dynamic range of the clarinet is the greatest of all the woodwinds; every note may be played loud or soft with little or no difficulty. Large intervals are easily slurred from low to high; slurring from high to low is more difficult. The clarinet cannot double tongue easily; so very fast tonguing is difficult. Fast tongued passages are often written in a "slur two tongue two" pattern or as a divided part with two players alternating measures, one playing while the other rests. The contra-alto and contrabass clarinets are best suited to sustained notes, as they can be sluggish and bulky sounding on quick passages.

Saxophones

The saxophone is similar to the clarinet in that it uses a single reed; but the shape of the tube is conical, producing a warm but slightly nasal sound. The saxophone is a modern instrument, invented in 1846 by Adolphe Sax. Unlike the other instruments, all the sizes of the saxophone were developed at one time; and the timbre of every saxophone is virtually the same throughout the ranges of each instrument.

The soprano saxophone, usually available at the professional level, can be found either straight or curved;

Saxophones:
(small to large)
soprano saxophone,
alto saxophone,
tenor saxophone,
baritone saxophone.

the straight model is more common. The alto, tenor, and baritone saxophones are the most common saxophones, and the bass saxophone is relatively rare, even among professionals.

The saxophone has a broad dynamic range, but it is most easily played loud. It has the same limitations with regard to articulation as does the clarinet.

Horns

The horn is a brass instrument with a narrow, conical-shaped tube. Most horns have 4 rotary valves; however, some horns have only three.

The early horns had no valves, and they were played in the upper range where the partials are close together. A few notes between the partials could be forced to sound by placing the hand deeper into the bell. An early horn player would use several horns, each pitched in a different key, depending on the music being played. Later, horns were made so a section of tubing could be replaced to change the key of the horn. Modern horns with four valves, called *double french horns*, contain the tubing of two three-valve horns, one pitched in F and the other in B-flat. The fourth valve, operated with the thumb, alternates the air stream between the two sets of tubing.

The lowest notes of the horn, not included in its normal range, are weak and dark. The characteristic timbre of the horn is produced in the uppermost two octaves. The timbre of the horn may be altered by stopping the end of the horn with the hand, producing a forceful brassy sound, or by using a mute, which produces a distant, buzzing sound.

The horn, like all the brass instruments, can have difficulty playing sudden leaps from the low range to the high range, because it can be difficult to pick out the correct partial to play in the high range. Because of the horn's rich timbre, slurred leaps will sound a bit like glissandos.

Trills may be executed by using the valves or by using only the lips to trill between two adjacent partials. In the same way, glissandos may be produced by using the valves or by slurring across the partials without using the valves, the latter being more effective on the horn.

Trumpets

The trumpet family is a set of instruments with cylindrical tubes and a cup-shaped mouthpiece. Most trumpets have three valves; occasionally a fourth valve is added to the piccolo trumpet.

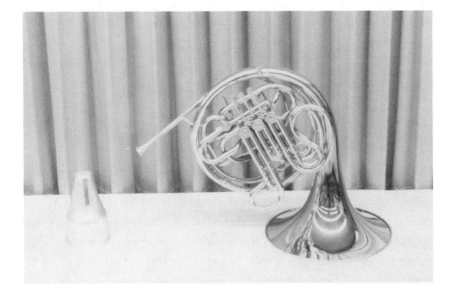

Horn, mute.

Trumpets:
B-flat trumpet *(left)*, C trumpet.
Mutes *(from the left)*: harmon,
plunger, cup, straight.

The modern, valved trumpet was developed from the valveless trumpet, an instrument used mostly for signals and fanfares until the eighteenth century. In the fifteenth century, to make the valveless trumpet more versatile, a straight slide was added; the player would hold the mouthpiece to his lips and slide the rest of the instrument up and down the length of the tube. The slide trumpet was used through the seventeenth century, where it was almost replaced by the *sackbutt*, the predecessor of the trombone. In the late eighteenth century, the slide trumpet became popular again, and over time the clumsy slide was replaced with valves to produce the modern trumpet.

Over the years, the trumpet has been made in at least thirteen different sizes; however, only a few are commonly used today. These are the piccolo trumpet, E-flat trumpet, C trumpet, and the B-flat trumpet.

The piccolo trumpet was designed to play Baroque trumpet parts easily. Due to the nature of the valveless trumpet, it had to be played in its highest range to obtain enough useful notes. By using a piccolo trumpet, which plays one octave higher than the regular trumpet, the normal range of the piccolo trumpet could be used instead of the extreme range of the regular trumpet to play Baroque music. The piccolo trumpet is relatively rare. The E-flat trumpet is also used for playing valveless trumpet parts of the late Baroque and early classical periods. It is usually available at the professional level.

The B-flat trumpet, the brass equivalent of the B-flat clarinet, is the most common trumpet. For playing orchestral music in sharp keys, the C trumpet was developed; however, it has a brighter tone than the B-flat instrument and may be substituted only when its bright tone is acceptable. Most professional players will have both instruments.

Larger trumpets called tenor and bass trumpets have been made, but they are rare. The bass trumpet is the same as the trombone in size and timbre, except that it has valves instead of slides. In fact, a bass trumpet shaped like a trombone is called a valve trombone.

The trumpet has a brilliant, blaring sound over its normal range, which begins at the second partial. The fundamental pitches, or pedal tones, are rarely used on the trumpet because they are weak and insecure due to the small bore of the instrument. These notes are not included in the normal range of the instrument. The trumpet has a good dynamic compass over its entire range except for the lowest notes which are difficult to play loudly, and the highest notes, which are difficult to play softly.

The trumpet can execute trills and slurs over large intervals slightly better than the horn can. A glissando using the valves usually sounds better than a slur across the partials without using the valves.

Several mutes are available to alter the timbre of the trumpet. The straight mute, used most often, makes the sound somewhat thin and distant. The harmon mute, which forces the sound through a small opening in a metal stem, produces a thin, metallic buzzing sound. The exact timbre of the sound may be adjusted by pulling the stem partially out of the mute or by removing it altogether. The hand may be moved in front of the mute to produce a "wa-wa" sound. The plunger mute, so called because it is the rubber end of the plumber's helper, is held in the player's left hand and manipulated over the bell to mute the instrument as desired. By opening and closing the bell with the mute, several syllables may be articulated. The cup mute is similar to a plunger, but it has a stem that holds it in place. It produces a very warm and woodwind-like sound.

Trombones

The trombone is acoustically identical to the trumpet, except that it uses a slide instead of valves to adjust the length of the tube. Most trombones also have one or two valves operated with the thumb, which give the instrument greater agility in the low range.

The trombone evolved from a Renaissance instrument called the *sackbutt*, which was virtually identical to the modern trombone except for its smaller diameter tubing and bell.

The trombone is available in two sizes, the (tenor) trombone and the bass trombone. The bass trombone has a larger bore than the tenor trombone, and it usually has two valves. These features make the bass trombone easier to play in the lowest range of the instrument but harder to play in the upper range. In overall length both instruments are the same.

The trombone has a powerful, clear sound. The tone may be altered with the same selection of mutes as for the trumpet. The harmon mute, however, is very expensive, and it will usually be found only at the professional level.

Because the trombone has a slide instead of valves,

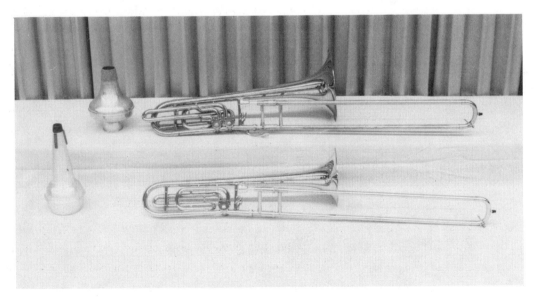

Trombones:
bass trombone *(top)*,
(tenor) trombone.
Mutes: harmon *(top)*,
straight.

glissandos are easy to produce. A very smooth glissando may be executed over an interval of a fifth, the range of the slide. A disadvantage of the slide is that a slurred passage must be slightly articulated so that the slide may be moved without producing a glissando between notes. Also, trills are much more difficult to execute on the trombone than on other brass instruments.

Tubas

The tuba family consists of instruments with a broad, conical bore. The common instruments included in the tuba family are the E-flat cornet, cornet, flügelhorn, baritone horn, euphonium, and tuba.

The cornet, usually associated with the trumpet, is a member of the tuba family because of its conical bore. The cornet evolved from a woodwind instrument called the *cornett*. Cornetts were made of wood and leather. They had fingerholes, but were played like brass instruments. The other members of the tuba family came about when valves were added to the military bugle. The conical shape of the tubas gives them a full, rich, mellow sound which fills the room even at low dynamic levels.

The cornets and flügelhorn are usually played by trumpet players; the music is written in the treble clef. They are usually available at the professional level. The baritone horn and euphonium have about the same range; but the euphonium has a larger bore, giving it a more resonant, melodious sound. The baritone and euphonium may be considered to be either non-transposing bass clef instruments or transposing treble clef instruments, depending on whether a trumpet player or a tuba player will be playing them.

The tuba is available in several sizes, pitched in several different keys. The selection of a particular size and key of tuba is left to the player, who transposes the part to the proper key as he plays. A special tuba called the *sousaphone* is available for marching band use.

All the instruments in the tuba family have an even timbre throughout their range. Despite their size, the tubas are very agile instruments, and runs, trills, and rapid passages are not difficult even on the largest tubas.

The timbre of the instruments may be changed by using a mute. The cornets and flügelhorn may use trumpet mutes, and straight mutes are available for the lower tubas. The tuba mute is very large and somewhat uncommon. Because the mute is so awkward to put into the bell, it is usually used for the entire duration of a movement.

Tubas:
(from the left) E-flat cornet, B-flat cornet, flügelhorn, baritone, euphonium, tuba, sousaphone, mute.

Percussion

The percussion instruments may be divided into three groups: the drums, the mallet instruments, and the *traps*, a catch-all category which includes everything from cymbals to whistles. Every drum listed here is available at the professional level; only the more common ones will be available to amateurs.

Drums. Drums consist of a membrane stretched across a frame. Included in this category are the tympani, tom toms, snare drum, bass drum, bongos and congas.

The tympani are the only drums which are tunable to a specific pitch; a pedal is used to change the tension on the head. The tympani are played with a variety of tympani sticks. Most ensembles will have a set of five tympani.

The tom toms have one head and are tunable to relative pitches from high to low. A variation of the tom tom, called the *rototom*, allows a player to change the pitch of the drum while playing by rotating the head of the drum. Tom toms are usually played in sets of four different sizes. A variety of sticks may be used to produce various sounds. A common effect

called the *rimshot* is produced by striking the head and the metal rim of the drum simultaneously.

Snare drums have two heads; the lower head has a number of wires stretched across it which slap back against the lower head whenever the drum is struck. A field drum is a snare drum with a longer shell and a lower pitch.

The bass drum is a double-headed drum without a snare, tuned to a low but indefinite pitch. A roll on the bass drum produces a powerful rumble which can give the impression of doubling the pitch of another instrument at a lower octave. The bongos and congas have a thick, single head on a wooden shell. The drums are usually played in pairs and struck with the hands or with sticks.

Mallet Instruments. The mallet instruments produce actual pitches. They are played with a variety of wooden or plastic mallets.

The chimes sound like large bells, and they are played by striking the tops of the tubes with a hammer. A pedal allows all the chime tubes to be damped at the same time.

The xylophone has rectangular bars made of hard wood or fiberglass, held in a wooden frame. The

Drums:
(back row) bass drum, crash cymbals, tympani,
(front row) snare drum, field drum, tom toms.

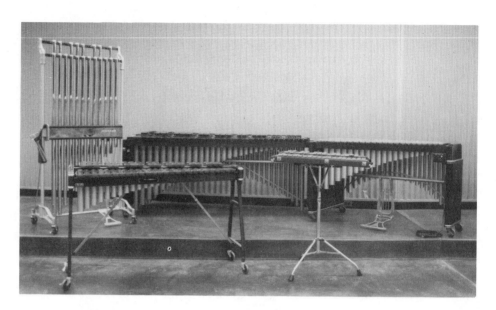

Mallets:
(back row) chimes,
marimba, vibraphone,
(front row) xylophone,
orchestra bells.

marimba is similar to the xylophone, except that the bars are made of softer wood in a slightly different shape, and they are played with softer mallets. The layout of the bars is the same as a piano keyboard, and a player can strike several bars at once by holding two or more mallets in each hand.

The vibraphone has bars made of metal and a vibrato mechanism which is operated by an electric motor. The speed of the vibrato may be changed with a speed control on the motor. Vibraphones have a damper pedal which stops the vibration of all the bars. They are usually played with soft mallets. Orchestra bells are a set of metal bars struck with plastic or brass mallets. The volume depends on the type of mallet used.

Traps. Any instrument which is not a drum or mallet instrument is included in this family of instruments. The commonly used traps are described here.

The tambourine consists of a thin shell with metal rattles which jingle against one another; it may have a head across one side of the shell. The tambourine may be shaken, struck with the hands or sticks, or rubbed with the thumb. Maracas, which are shaken in pairs, are hollow, gourd-shaped bulbs containing beans. The cabasa has strings of metal beads which slide over a corrugated metal surface to produce a grinding sound. The vibraslap is an instrument which vibrates when the ball end is struck with the hand. The wooden sounding end has some loose metal rivets which rattle against the sounding board as the springy metal frame vibrates. The ratchet consists of a hand cranked cogwheel and wooden slats which snap against it, all in a metal frame. The güiro, or gourd scraper, is a fish-shaped wooden rasp which is played by scraping a stick across parallel grooves. Sand blocks are pieces of wood covered with sandpaper which are rubbed against one another.

Sleigh bells consist of a handle with a number of spherical bells attached to it. The bell tree is a nested set of untuned bells upon which glissandos are played with brass mallets. Brake drums, from the automobile junkyard, are struck with mallets and produce a surprisingly resonant "bonk" sound. They are usually played in sets of three or four different sizes. Antique cymbals are small thick metal disks which are struck against one another producing an untuned bell-like sound. Triangles are bent metal rods hung by a string and played with a metal beater. The size of the triangle determines the relative pitch, and the

diameter of the beater determines the volume. Agogo bells are made of two cone-shaped bells on a bent metal rod. They are struck with a wooden stick and have a dry "clanking" sound. Cowbells are available in several sizes and are played with a wooden stick to produce a "clank" sound. The flexatone is a hand held adaptation of the musical saw, consisting of a springy piece of metal which is struck by rubber balls when it is shaken. The pitch of the instrument is altered by bending the metal sheet.

Windchimes consist of hanging objects which strike against one another. They are usually suspended and played with the hands. The objects which rattle may be glass, wood, metal, bamboo, or shell. A special kind of windchime, called the *Mark tree*, has a single row of tubes of increasing length which produce a shimmering effect when played by sweeping them with the hand.

Castanets are disk-shaped plastic clappers hinged to a wooden block. The whip or slapstick is made from two slats of wood which are hinged together at one end. The claves are a pair of hardwood sticks which are struck together to produce a rich click. Wood blocks are hollow wood boxes which are struck with sticks. Temple blocks are actually wooden bells, usu-

ally in a set of five pitches, which approximate the pentatonic scale.

Cymbals are disks of spun brass; the thickness and size of a cymbal determines the relative pitch and timbre. Suspended cymbals are held on a stand and are played with mallets or sticks, while crash cymbals are held with handles and played by striking one cymbal against the other with a glancing blow. Gongs and tam tams are large disks of heavy metal with a bent rim. The two instruments are often confused with one another. Gongs have a raised dome in the center and a very wide rim, and are available in many different sizes. The tam tam, on the other hand, is a larger, flat disk with a narrow rim and less definite pitch. The tam tam is the more common instrument, and it is often used even when a gong is specified.

A number of novelty items, ranging from dimestore toys to specialized instruments, are used in modern music. The more common novelty items are the duck call, the slide whistle, the water filled "nightingale" whistle, the police whistle, the pop gun, and the mouth siren.

Trap Set. The trap set is a collection of percussion instruments designed to be played simultaneously

Trap set.

while the player sits on a stool. The instruments included in the trap set will vary; a basic trap set contains a foot operated bass drum, high hat cymbals, suspended cymbal, snare drum, tom tom, and floor tom. Additional instruments may be added as needed.

Keyboard Instruments

Included in the classification of keyboard instruments are the piano, organ, harpsichord, and celesta. These instruments are unrelated except for the method of playing them.

Piano. The piano is by far the most popular keyboard instrument. The piano produces sound when a felt hammer strikes the strings. The lowest octave has one string for each note, the next octave has two strings for each note, and the remaining octaves have three strings for each note. When the key is released, a damper stops the vibration of the strings. The volume depends on how fast the key is depressed.

Most pianos sold in America have three pedals to aid in playing. The damper pedal raises all the dampers away from the strings, allowing a note to sustain after the key is released. Using the damper pedal also produces a richer sound quality because of

sympathetic vibration from the other related strings. The soft pedal, or una corda pedal, shifts the action and hammers to the right, so that only two of the three strings in the mid and high range are struck, producing a softer sound. The sostenuto pedal on a grand piano holds selected dampers up while the rest of the dampers operate normally. After a key is depressed, the sostenuto pedal is depressed; and the damper for that particular note will be held up until the pedal is released. On upright pianos and low quality grand pianos the sostenuto pedal is simply a damper pedal which affects only the bass clef notes.

On the keyboard, a typical pianist can span one octave between his thumb and little finger. Because of the mechanics of the piano, notes may be played loud or soft with a variety of articulations.

Organ. The organ is the largest and most complex of all the instruments. This section applies to all fine organs, both pipe organs and electronic organs, typically found in large churches and concert halls.

The organ console, from which the instrument is played, usually contains two or three keyboards for the hands called the *manuals*, a keyboard for the feet called the *pedals*, various knobs or tabs called *stops*,

Electronic organ.

and pedals to control the volume. The manuals are named from top to bottom: the *swell organ*, *great organ*, and *choir organ*. Some consoles have four or more manuals; the additional manuals have names such as *solo* or *bombard*. The stops are used to engage various ranks of pipes with the various keyboards. The volume and timbre of the organ is determined by the number of stops engaged. The ranks of pipes for the swell stops on nineteenth and early twentieth century organs are contained in a box with louvers which may be opened and closed with a pedal to give some dynamic and timbral control. Earlier mechanical organs rely only on combinations of stops for volume changes. The electronic organ is equipped with volume pedals for all the keyboards.

Hundreds of different stops have been made for various organs; the exact *disposition* of a particular organ depends on the organ maker. Each stop engages a set of pipes with a particular characteristic sound. The electronic organ creates the various sounds with either an analog or digital circuit and plays the sound through a loudspeaker system. To engage a particular rank of pipes, a player actuates (pulls) the stop for that particular rank. Most organs with electronic actions are equipped with pistons, which are pushbuttons that allow a player to preset a selection of stops; so when the piston is pressed, the selected stops are engaged and all the other stops are disengaged. An organ usually has several different pistons located all over the organ. A *crescendo pedal* allows the player to slowly engage all the stops that are not already pulled in a smooth, graded series by rocking the pedal forward. As the pedal is rocked back, all the stops will be disengaged in reverse order, leaving only the stops that were previously pulled. A *tutti* stop engages all the stops at one time.

The relative pitch of the pipes in a particular stop is determined by the length in feet of the longest pipe in the rank. An 8' stop will sound as written, a 4' stop will sound one octave higher, and a 2' stop will sound two octaves higher. Similarly, a 16' stop will sound one octave lower, and a 32' stop will sound two octaves lower. Stops which play at intervals other than an octave, usually a perfect fifth higher than written, are called *mutations* and have fractional lengths. To designate a particular stop, the name is specified, followed by the length (i.e. flutes 4').

A characteristic of the organ is that, unlike the piano, a note sounds only as long as a key is depressed. Organists develop fingering techniques which are quite

This outline describes the various stops which may be found on pipe organs and fine electronic organs. The actual number and type of stops available on a particular organ will vary greatly depending on the organ maker.

Flue stops - open pipes that produce sound in the same manner as the recorder. The sound begins with a characteristic "chiff" as the air rushes into the pipe. The electronic organ often has a feature to imitates the "chiff" sound.

    Foundations - the most common stops, they produce the typical organ sound. Their timbre blends well with any other stop.

        Diapason Chorus - the basic stops on every organ; they are available in length from 64' to 1/2'.

        Mixtures - engage two or more carefully tuned ranks of foundations simultaneously to produce a special sound.

    Flute Stops - available in length from 32' to 1/2'. The number and size of these stops will vary from organ to organ.

        Open Flutes - sound very much like the recorder.

        Stopped Flutes - soft in volume and sound somewhat hooty.

        Half Stopped Flutes - also soft, but shrill and penetrating.

    String Stops - available in length from 32' to 2'. They have a bright, string-like tone and are named after the various string instruments.

Reed Stops - the pitch is produced by a metal reed. The pipe is only a resonator; its shape and length affect the timbre but not the pitch.

    Chorus Reeds - very loud and brilliant pipes available in length from 32' to 4'. They are named after the brass instruments.

    Semichorus Reeds - soft and buzzy, named after the Renaissance instruments. They are available in length from 32' to 1'.

    Imitative Reeds - a nineteenth century addition to imitate the sounds of the bassoon, oboe, and clarinet. They are available in length from 32' to 4' and are named after the instrument which they imitate.

Diaphone Stops - a specialized foundation stop that uses a dish-shaped reed that plays very loudly. They are available in 64', 32', and 16' lengths.

Tremulant - not a rank of pipes, but a stop that causes the air supply to fluctuate, producing a vibrato on all of the stops.

Pipe Organ and Electronic Organ Stops

different from traditional piano fingering to play legato passages.

The pedals are played with the feet, using both the toe and heel. Black keys are played only with the toe; trills require both feet. To aid in playing moving passages the toe may be slid from a black key to any adjacent key, and the foot may be walked up the keys, alternating from toe to heel. In addition, the toe may be exchanged for the heel, and one foot may be exchanged for the other while sustaining a single note. One foot may also play any two side-by-side pedals.

Harpsichord. The harpsichord was in use by the fifteenth century and was prominent during the seventeenth and eighteenth centuries. Modern reproductions of harpsichords are occasionally used in contemporary music in addition to their use in Baroque music.

The harpsichord produces sound when a depressed key lifts a jack with a quill which plucks a string. When the key is released, a damper stops the vibration of the string. Because of the action, changes in dynamics are not possible.

A harpsichord may have one or two keyboards, sometimes with several sets of strings available for each one. Pedals are used to engage the various sets of strings (usually 4' and 8'; occasionally 16') with the keyboards, and sometimes a pedal can be used to link the upper and lower keyboards so that both are played when a key is depressed on the lower keyboard.

A variety of techniques are used by harpsichord players to produce different sounds. For example, by arpeggiating the chords at various speeds a volume difference can be heard; slow arpeggios will sound softer than fast arpeggios, and a non-arpeggiated chord will sound accented.

Celesta. The celesta is essentially a set of orchestra bells which are struck by hammers connected to a keyboard. The hammer will strike the bell harder if the key is pressed faster. A damper stops the notes after the key is released, unless the damper pedal is depressed. Because the celesta is very expensive, many ensembles, both amateur and professional, use a digital synthesizer to create the sound of the celesta electronically.

Harp

The harp has seven strings per octave, one for each diatonic pitch. Each of the pitches, in all the octaves, is controlled by one of seven pedals which move fork-shaped tuning pegs against the strings, al-

Harpsichord.

Harp.

lowing each string to be sharp, natural, or flat, depending on the position of the pedals. The pedals may be set to allow the harp to play all the notes in a given key, or they may be set to produce enharmonic pitches, allowing all the strings to be tuned to as few as four different pitches. The strings may also be tuned to pentatonic or whole tone scales.

The harp is held on the player's right shoulder, and the hands play the strings from opposite sides. The left hand plays the bass strings, and the right hand plays the treble strings. Because the little finger is not used, only four notes may be played simultaneously with each hand. The hand can span about one octave.

Violins

The instruments of the violin family have four strings which are usually played with a bow. The bow is made from the tail hair of specially bred horses. The bridge and fingerboard are curved so that the inner strings can be bowed singly. Also, two adjacent strings may be played at the same time.

The violin family has three members, the violin, viola, and cello. The string bass, a member of the *viol* family, is usually included in the violin family for convenience, even though it is not a true violin. The violin and viola are held between the chin and left shoulder, and the cello and string bass are held vertically.

The strings of the violin, viola, and cello are tuned in perfect fifths from the lowest note; the string bass strings are tuned in perfect fourths from the lowest note. Some string basses have a fifth string which is tuned to low C.

The violins are usually played with vibrato. This effect is created by pinching the string against the fingerboard and rocking the finger back and forth to alter the pitch slightly.

A mute may be attached to the bridge of the violins; it softens the volume and makes the sound slightly distant. The mute works by making the bridge heavier and less efficient in transmitting the vibration of the string to the body of the instrument.

A variety of articulations may be produced by plucking the strings with the finger, striking the string with the wood of the bow, or playing with different bowing techniques.

Voice

The major difference between instrumental and vocal music is the addition of text to the music. This section will briefly discuss the ranges of different voices and diction, which is the setting of the text to the music.

Every voice is different, but each can generally be placed into one of four categories, depending on the range of the voice. The higher women's voice is called the *soprano*. The sopranos may be divided into first and second soprano; the second sopranos, sometimes called *mezzo-sopranos*, will tend to have more depth to their voice in the lower range but will not have quite the high range of the first sopranos. The lower women's voice is called the *alto*. Like the soprano, the altos may be divided into the first and second parts. Men's voices are also divided high and low; the high voice is called the *tenor* and the low voice is called the *bass*. Traditional four part writing has a part for soprano, alto, tenor, and bass. Three additional categories are used to describe special voices which do not fall into any of the normal ranges. A man's voice which falls between the tenor and bass is called a *baritone*. The baritone would have difficulty singing very high tenor parts and very low bass parts. A tenor who can sing very high, with the same range as an alto, is called a *countertenor*; and an alto who can sing very low, with the same range as a tenor, is called a *contralto*. Children, both boys and girls, can sing about the same range as the alto.

Diction refers to the pronunciation and enunciation of words which are sung. The natural flow of the words and the emphasis of particular vowel and consonant sounds must be considered when setting a text to music. The natural accents of the text are usually placed on accented syllables at a point in the melodic line that would receive an accent naturally, such as the first beat of a measure.

The different syllables in a word can be divided into several categories, based on their vowel sound. Consonants are used only to begin and end a particular vowel sound. A vowel sound may be one of the five primary vowels, a secondary vowel, a *diphthong*, which is a combination of two vowel sounds, or a *triphthong*, which is a combination of three vowel sounds.

The primary vowel sounds are the "a" sound in "date," the "e" sound in "feet," the "ah" sound in "hot," the "o" sound in "obey," and the "oo" sound in "boot." All the other pure vowel sounds are secondary vowels. The vowel pair "ou" is almost always a diphthong. To obtain the best diction, sustain only words with primary vowel sounds. Occasionally a secondary vowel sound may be sustained, however it will not sound good. Never try to sustain a diphthong or triphthong. Studying examples of choral works is probably the best way to learn proper diction.

Violins:
(small to large) violin, viola, cello, string bass.

Appendix B
Music Theory

This appendix covers basic principles of music theory. A knowledge of music theory fundamentals is assumed; therefore, this appendix was designed to serve as a review and reference rather than a course in music theory.

1. Fundamentals of Music Theory

Note and Rest Values

The following table is based on a quarter note receiving one beat:

Quarter Note Beats	American Name	British Name	Note Symbol	Rest Symbol
8	Double Whole	Breve		
4	Whole	Semibreve		
2	Half	Minim		
1	Quarter	Crotchet		
$^1/_2$	Eighth	Quaver		
$^1/_4$	Sixteenth	Semiquaver		
$^1/_8$	Thirty-second	Demisemiquaver		
$^1/_{16}$	Sixty-fourth	Hemidemisemiquaver		

Meter

In *simple meter* each beat may be divided into two parts and subdivided into four parts. In *compound meter* each beat may be divided into three parts and subdivided into six parts.

Simple Meter:

Compound Meter:

The *meter signature* is written as two numbers, one over the other; it is not a fraction. In simple meter the upper number gives the number of beats in a measure and the lower number tells what fraction of a whole note receives the beat. In compound meter the upper number divided by three gives the number of beats in the measure, and the lower number tells what fraction of a whole note will receive one-third of a beat.

simple duple	$\frac{2}{8}$	$\frac{2}{4}$	$\frac{2}{2}$		*compound duple*	$\frac{6}{8}$	$\frac{6}{4}$	$\frac{6}{2}$
simple triple	$\frac{3}{8}$	$\frac{3}{4}$	$\frac{3}{2}$		*compound triple*	$\frac{9}{8}$	$\frac{9}{4}$	$\frac{9}{2}$
simple quadruple	$\frac{4}{8}$	$\frac{4}{4}$	$\frac{4}{2}$		*compound quadruple*	$\frac{12}{8}$	$\frac{12}{4}$	$\frac{12}{2}$

Complex or *asymmetric* meters are combinations of duple and triple meters.

$$\frac{5}{4} = \frac{3}{4} + \frac{2}{4} \text{ or } \frac{2}{4} + \frac{3}{4}$$

$$\frac{7}{4} = \frac{2}{4} + \frac{2}{4} + \frac{3}{4} \text{ or } \frac{2}{4} + \frac{3}{4} + \frac{2}{4} \text{ or } \frac{3}{4} + \frac{2}{4} + \frac{2}{4}$$

$$\frac{8}{8} = \frac{3}{8} + \frac{3}{8} + \frac{2}{8} \text{ or } \frac{3}{8} + \frac{2}{8} + \frac{3}{8} \text{ or } \frac{2}{8} + \frac{3}{8} + \frac{3}{8}$$

Borrowed division occurs when a figure from simple meter is used in compound meter, or a figure from compound meter is used in simple meter.

Simple Meter ("triplets" and "double triplets" are borrowed):

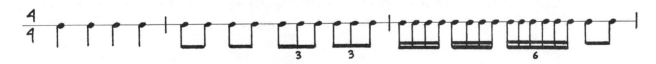

Compound Meter ("duples" and "quadruples" are borrowed):

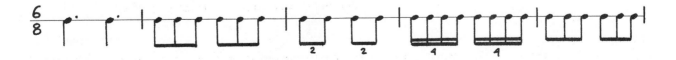

Clefs

In the example below "middle C" is shown in relation to all the clef signs. Of the clefs shown only the treble, bass, alto, and tenor clefs are commonly used.

Pitch Names

The notes are normally referred to by letter names only. If stating the octave of the pitch is necessary, use the following system to indicate each pitch and octave.

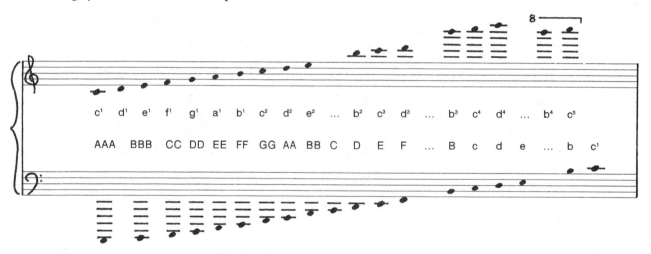

Accidentals and Enharmonic Equivalents

A sharp raises a pitch by a half step, a double sharp raises a pitch by a whole step, a flat lowers a pitch by a half step, and a double flat lowers a pitch by a whole step. Accidentals used to establish a particular scale may be placed in a *key signature*.

sharp: ♯   double sharp: 𝄪   flat: ♭   double flat: ♭♭   key signature:

If two notes have different names but are of the same pitch, such as f-sharp and g-flat, they are called *enharmonic equivalents*. When considering music from a theoretical standpoint, remember that although the notes may sound the same, they serve different functions harmonically and cannot be used interchangeably.

2. Scales and Keys

Diatonic Scales

The major and natural minor scales used in most Western music are diatonic scales. These scales are two of seven *church modes* first developed by the Greeks (but in a different form and with different names) based on a mathematical sequence of frequencies. All the diatonic modes are made up of whole and half steps; the pattern is the same as the pattern of white keys on the piano.

The natural modes (played only on the white keys of the piano) are summarized below.

Name	Range on the White Keys	Pattern of Whole and Half Steps
Ionian (major)	C to C	W W H W W W H
Dorian	D to D	W H W W W H W
Phrygian	E to E	H W W W H W W
Lydian	F to F	W W W H W W H
Mixolydian	G to G	W W H W W H W
Aeolian (minor)	A to A	W H W W H W W
Locrian	B to B	H W W H W W W

Any of the modes may be transposed to begin on any starting note. Use accidentals or a key signature to retain the pattern of whole and half steps.

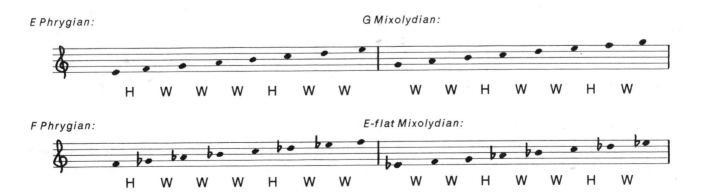

E Phrygian: H W W W H W W

G Mixolydian: W W H W W H W

F Phrygian: H W W W H W W

E-flat Mixolydian: W W H W W H W

Major and Minor Scales

The major scale is the same as the Ionian mode. The natural minor scale is the same as the Aeolian mode. Accidentals are added to retain the pattern of whole and half steps when transposing the scales to begin on a particular starting note. The following table shows the keynotes of the various major and minor scales for the various key signatures.

Sharps and flats are added in a specific sequence based on the interval of a fifth. Thus, if the chart calls for three sharps, the sharps are the first three in the list of sharps. Key signatures of greater than seven sharps or flats are not shown; such keys are theoretical and require double sharps or double flats in the key signature.

Order of Sharps:	F	C	G	D	A	E	B
Order of Flats:	B	E	A	D	G	C	F

KEY SIGNATURE	MAJOR SCALE	MINOR SCALE
7 sharps	C-sharp	a-sharp
6 sharps	F-sharp	d-sharp
5 sharps	B	g-sharp
4 sharps	E	c-sharp
3 sharps	A	f-sharp
2 sharps	D	b
1 sharp	G	e
NONE	C	a
1 flat	F	d
2 flats	B-flat	g
3 flats	E-flat	c
4 flats	A-flat	f
5 flats	D-flat	b-flat
6 flats	G-flat	e-flat
7 flats	C-flat	a-flat

Each degree of the scale is given a name based on its harmonic function.

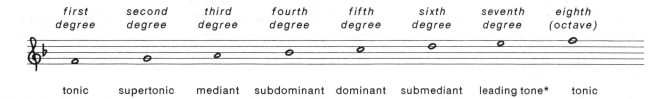

first degree	second degree	third degree	fourth degree	fifth degree	sixth degree	seventh degree	eighth (octave)
tonic	supertonic	mediant	subdominant	dominant	submediant	leading tone*	tonic

in the natural minor scale, the seventh degree is called the subtonic.

The minor scale is usually altered to make it more useful in harmony. In the natural form the minor scale lacks a leading tone; the seventh degree is a whole step below the tonic. Because the leading tone serves such an important function in Western harmony, the seventh degree of the scale is often raised one half step, both ascending and descending, to produce the *harmonic minor* scale.

By raising the seventh degree of the scale one half step, the interval of an *augmented second* (1¹/₂ steps) is created between the sixth and seventh degrees of the scale. This large interval does not lend itself to a smooth melody, so another scale, the melodic minor scale, may be used for melodic passages. To create the *melodic minor* scale, the sixth and seventh degree are raised on the ascending scale. The descending scale is the same as the natural minor.

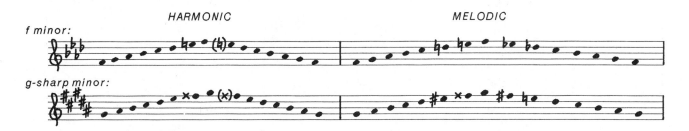

Two terms are used to describe the relationship between major and minor scales. A major and minor scale which share the same starting note are called *parallel*, and a major and minor scale which share the same key signature are called *relative*.

Non-Diatonic Scales

The *chromatic scale* is composed of all half steps. Since no particular note is perceived as the tonic, the scale may start and end on any note. The chromatic scale is usually written with sharps when ascending and flats when descending to minimize the need for natural signs.

The *whole tone scale* consists of only whole steps. Like the chromatic scale it has no apparent tonality. Two whole tone scales may be written, one that contains C-natural and one that contains C-sharp.

The *pentatonic scale* contains five tones. The pattern of whole and half steps is the same as that of the black keys on the piano. Shown below is the natural pentatonic scale. Like any of the diatonic scales, it may be transposed to other keys by maintaining the proper intervals between the notes.

3. Intervals

Analysis of Intervals

An *interval* is the melodic distance between two notes. The analysis of an interval consists of two parts, the number of notes between the pitches, and the quality of the interval. Without regard to quality, the intervals from unison to octave are shown below.

| unison | second | third | fourth | fifth | sixth | seventh | octave |

Intervals of a unison, fourth, fifth, and octave are called *perfect* intervals, and intervals of a second, third, sixth, and seventh are called *major/minor* intervals. Intervals from the tonic to any other degree of the major scale are either perfect or major. If the interval has been altered so that it is smaller or larger than the perfect or major interval, the quality is changed as follows:

	Perfect Intervals (1, 4, 5, 8)	*Major/minor Intervals* (2, 3, 6, 7)
2 half steps larger	double augmented (AA)	double augmented (AA)
1 half step larger	augmented (A)	augmented (A)
Interval as written	**Perfect (P)**	**Major (M)**
1 half step smaller	diminished (d)	minor (m)
2 half steps smaller	double diminished (dd)	diminished (d)

Two methods may be used to determine the quality of intervals. The first method requires three steps:

- Count the distance between the two notes.
- Construct a major scale based on the lower note of the interval.
- Analyze the quality of the interval based on its relation to the major scale.

Example 1:

Given: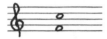

1. **Count the distance between the notes:**
   F to G to A to B to C = 5

2. **Construct a major scale on the lower note:**

3. **Analyze the interval:**
   "C" is a member of the F major scale, so the interval is a "perfect fifth."

Example 2:

Given:

1. **Count the distance between the notes:**
   E to F to G to A to B to C = 6

2. **Construct a major scale on the lower note:**

3. **Analyze the interval:**
   "C-sharp" is a member of the E major scale, so the interval is a "major sixth."

Example 3:

Given: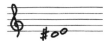

1. **Count the distance between the notes:**
   D to E = 2

2. **Construct a major scale on the lower note:**

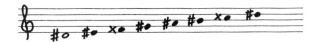

3. **Analyze the interval:**
   "E" is not a member of the D-sharp major scale, so the interval has been altered. The interval is one-half step smaller than a major second, therefore it is a "minor second."

Example 4:

Given: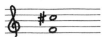

1. **Count the distance between the notes:**
   F to G to A to B to C = 5

2. **Construct a major scale on the lower note:**

3. **Analyze the interval:**
   "C-sharp" is not a member of the F major scale, so the interval has been altered. The interval is one-half step larger than a perfect fifth, therefore it is an "augmented fifth."

The second method of analyzing intervals involves counting the number of half steps in the interval to determine its quality. The table below shows the number of half steps in the perfect, major, and minor intervals. The interval of an augmented fourth or diminished fifth is often referred to as a *tritone* (*tri* = three, *tone* = whole step).

HALF STEPS	QUALITY
0	P1
1	m2
2	M2
3	m3
4	M3
5	P4
6	A4/d5
7	P5
8	m6
9	M6
10	m7
11	M7
12	P8

Diminished and augmented intervals are extrapolated from the table based on how many half steps the interval has been altered. Moving down on the table *augments* the interval, and moving up on the table *diminishes* it. For example, an augmented third contains 5 half steps, and a diminished seventh contains 9 half steps. The steps required for this method are shown in the examples.

Example 1:

Given: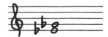

1. Count the distance between the notes:
   E to F to G = 3

2. Count the number of half steps:
   E-flat to E to F to G-flat = 3 half steps

3. Determine the quality of the interval from the chart:
   3 half step = "minor third"

Example 2:

Given: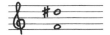

1. **Count the distance between the notes:**
   F to G to A to B to C to D = 6

2. **Count the number of half steps:**
   F to F-sharp to G to G-sharp to A to A-sharp to B to C to C-sharp to D to D-sharp = 10 half steps

3. **Determine the quality of the interval from the chart:**
   10 half steps = "minor seventh." But the interval is a sixth, so the quality must be extrapolated. Moving down on the chart one half step from the major sixth autments the interval, therefore the interval is an "augmented sixth."

Example 3:

Given: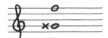

1. **Count the distance between the notes:**
   G to A to B to C to D to E to F = 7

2. **Count the number of half steps:**
   G-double sharp to A-sharp to B to C to C-sharp to D to D-sharp to E to F = 8 half steps

3. **Determine the quality of the interval from the chart:**
   8 half steps = "minor sixth." But the interval is a seventh, so the quality must be extrapolated. Moving up on the chart two half steps from the minor seventh diminishes the interval twice, therefore the interval is a "double diminished seventh."

On the following page is a chart which gives the quality of any interval. The lower note is found on the left side of the chart, and the upper note is found along the top of the chart; the quality of the interval is given by the intersection of the row and column. Do not rely on this chart to analyze intervals; use it only to verify the analysis done using one of the two methods described earlier.

QUALITIES OF INTERVALS

UPPER NOTE

LOWER NOTE	C♭♭	C♭	C	C#	Cx	D♭♭	D♭	D	D#	Dx	E♭♭	E♭	E	E#	Ex
C♭♭	P1	A1	**AA1**	3A1	4A1	M2	A2	**AA2**	3A2	4A2	M3	A3	**AA3**	3A3	4A3
C♭	d8	P1	**A1**	AA1	3A1	m2	M2	**A2**	AA2	3A2	m3	M3	**A3**	2A3	3A3
C	**dd8**	**d8**	**P1**	**A1**	**AA1**	**d2**	**m2**	**M2**	**A2**	**AA2**	**d3**	**m3**	**M3**	**A3**	**AA3**
C#	3d8	dd8	**d8**	P1	A1	dd2	d2	**m2**	M2	A2	dd3	d3	**m3**	M3	A3
Cx	4d8	3d8	**dd8**	d8	P1	3d2	dd2	**d2**	m2	M2	3d3	dd3	**d3**	m3	M3
D♭♭	m7	M7	**A7**	AA7	3A7	P1	A1	**AA1**	3A1	4A1	M2	A2	**AA2**	3A2	4A2
D♭	d7	m7	**M7**	A7	AA7	d8	P1	**A1**	AA1	3A1	m2	M2	**A2**	AA2	3A2
D	**dd7**	**d7**	**m7**	**M7**	**A7**	**dd8**	**d8**	**P1**	**A1**	**AA1**	**d2**	**m2**	**M2**	**A2**	**AA2**
D#	3d7	dd7	**d7**	m7	M7	3d8	dd8	**d8**	P1	A1	dd2	d2	**m2**	M2	A2
Dx	4d7	3d7	**dd7**	d7	m7	4d8	3d8	**dd8**	d8	P1	3d2	dd2	**d2**	m2	M2
E♭♭	m6	M6	**A6**	AA6	3A6	m7	M7	**A7**	AA7	3A7	P1	A1	**AA1**	3A1	4A1
E♭	d6	m6	**M6**	A6	AA6	d7	m7	**M7**	A7	AA7	d8	P1	**A1**	AA1	3A1
E	**dd6**	**d6**	**m6**	**M6**	**A6**	**dd7**	**d7**	**m7**	**M7**	**A7**	**dd8**	**d8**	**P1**	**A1**	**AA1**
E#	3d6	dd6	**d6**	m6	M6	3d7	dd7	**d7**	m7	M7	3d8	dd8	**d8**	P1	A1
Ex	4d6	3d6	**dd6**	d6	m6	4d7	3d7	**dd7**	d7	m7	4d8	3d8	**dd8**	d8	P1
F♭♭	P5	A5	**AA5**	3A5	4A5	M6	A6	**AA6**	3A6	4A6	M7	A7	**AA7**	3A7	4A7
F♭	d5	P5	**A5**	AA5	3A5	m6	M6	**A6**	AA6	3A6	m7	M7	**A7**	AA7	3A7
F	**dd5**	**d5**	**P5**	**A5**	**AA5**	**d6**	**m6**	**M6**	**A6**	**AA6**	**d7**	**m7**	**M7**	**A7**	**AA7**
F#	3d5	dd5	**d5**	P5	A5	dd6	d6	**m6**	M6	A6	dd7	d7	**m7**	M7	A7
Fx	4d5	3d5	**dd5**	d5	P5	3d6	dd6	**d6**	m6	M6	3d7	dd7	**d7**	m7	M7
G♭♭	P4	A4	**AA4**	3A4	4A4	P5	A5	**AA5**	3A5	4A5	M6	A6	**AA6**	3A6	4A6
G♭	d4	P4	**A4**	AA4	3A4	d5	P5	**A5**	AA5	3A5	m6	M6	**A6**	AA6	3A6
G	**dd4**	**d4**	**P4**	**A4**	**AA4**	**dd5**	**d5**	**P5**	**A5**	**AA5**	**d6**	**m6**	**M6**	**A6**	**AA6**
G#	3d4	dd4	**d4**	P4	A4	3d5	dd5	**d5**	P5	A5	dd6	d6	**m6**	M6	A6
Gx	4d4	3d4	**dd4**	d4	P4	4d5	3d5	**dd5**	d5	P5	3d6	dd6	**d6**	m6	M6
A♭♭	m3	M3	**A3**	AA3	3A3	P4	A4	**AA4**	3A4	4A4	P5	A5	**AA5**	3A5	4A5
A♭	d3	m3	**M3**	A3	AA3	d4	P4	**A4**	AA4	3A4	d5	P5	**A5**	AA5	3A5
A	**dd3**	**d3**	**m3**	**M3**	**A3**	**dd4**	**d4**	**P4**	**A4**	**AA4**	**dd5**	**d5**	**P5**	**A5**	**AA5**
A#	3d3	dd3	**d3**	m3	M3	3d4	dd4	**d4**	P4	A4	3d5	dd5	**d5**	P5	A5
Ax	4d3	3d3	**dd3**	d3	m3	4d4	3d4	**dd4**	d4	P4	4d5	3d5	**dd5**	d5	P5
B♭♭	m2	M2	**A2**	AA2	3A2	m3	M3	**A3**	AA3	3A3	P4	A4	**AA4**	3A4	4A4
B♭	d2	m2	**M2**	A2	AA2	d3	m3	**M3**	A3	AA3	d4	P4	**A4**	AA4	3A4
B	**dd2**	**d2**	**m2**	**M2**	**A2**	**dd3**	**d3**	**m3**	**M3**	**A3**	**dd4**	**d4**	**P4**	**A4**	**AA4**
B#	3d2	dd2	**d2**	m2	M2	3d3	dd3	**d3**	m3	M3	3d4	dd4	**d4**	P4	A4
Bx	4d2	3d2	**dd2**	d2	m2	4d3	3d3	**dd3**	d3	m3	4d4	3d4	**dd4**	d4	P4

KEY: 3A = triple augmented AA = double augmented A = augmented P = Perfect
M = major m = minor d = diminished dd = double diminished 3d = triple diminished

UPPER NOTE

	F♭♭	F♭	F	F#	Fx	G♭♭	G♭	G	G#	Gx	A♭♭	A♭	A	A#	Ax	B♭♭	B♭	B	B#	Bx
C♭♭	P4	A4	**AA4**	3A4	4A4	P5	A5	**AA5**	3A5	4A5	M6	A6	**AA6**	3A6	4A6	M7	A7	**AA7**	3A7	4A7
C♭	d4	P4	**A4**	AA4	3A4	d5	P5	**A5**	AA5	3A5	m6	M6	**A6**	AA6	3A6	m7	M7	**A7**	AA7	3A7
C	**dd4**	**d4**	**P4**	**A4**	**AA4**	**dd5**	**d5**	**P5**	**A5**	**AA5**	**d6**	**m6**	**M6**	**A6**	**AA6**	**d7**	**m7**	**M7**	**A7**	**AA7**
C#	3d4	dd4	**d4**	P4	A4	3d5	dd5	**d5**	P5	A5	dd6	d6	**m6**	M6	A6	dd7	d7	**m7**	M7	A7
Cx	4d4	3d4	**dd4**	d4	P4	4d5	3d5	**dd5**	d5	P5	3d6	dd6	**d6**	m6	M6	3d7	dd7	**d7**	m7	M7
D♭♭	m3	M3	**A3**	AA3	3A3	P4	A4	**AA4**	3A4	4A4	P5	A5	**AA5**	3A5	4A5	M6	A6	**AA6**	3A6	4A6
D♭	d3	m3	**M3**	A3	AA3	d4	P4	**A4**	AA4	3A4	d5	P5	**A5**	AA5	3A5	m6	M6	**A6**	AA6	3A6
D	**dd3**	**d3**	**m3**	**M3**	**A3**	**dd4**	**d4**	**P4**	**A4**	**AA4**	**dd5**	**d5**	**P5**	**A5**	**AA5**	**d6**	**m6**	**M6**	**A6**	**AA6**
D#	3d3	dd3	**d3**	m3	M3	3d4	dd4	**d4**	P4	A4	3d5	dd5	**d5**	P5	A5	dd6	d6	**m6**	M6	A6
Dx	4d3	3d3	**dd3**	d3	m3	4d4	3d4	**dd4**	d4	P4	4d5	3d5	**dd5**	d5	P5	3d6	dd6	**d6**	m6	M6
E♭♭	m2	M2	**A2**	AA2	3A2	m3	M3	**A3**	AA3	3A3	P4	A4	**AA4**	3A4	4A4	P5	A5	**AA5**	3A5	4A5
E♭	d2	m2	**M2**	A2	AA2	d3	m3	**M3**	A3	AA3	d4	P4	**A4**	AA4	3A4	d5	P5	**A5**	AA5	3A5
E	**dd2**	**d2**	**m2**	**M2**	**A2**	**dd3**	**d3**	**m3**	**M3**	**A3**	**dd4**	**d4**	**P4**	**A4**	**AA4**	**dd5**	**d5**	**P5**	**A5**	**AA5**
E#	3d2	dd2	**d2**	m2	M2	3d3	dd3	**d3**	m3	M3	3d4	dd4	**d4**	P4	A4	3d5	dd5	**d5**	P5	A5
Ex	4d2	3d2	**dd2**	d2	m2	4d3	3d3	**dd3**	d3	m3	4d4	3d4	**dd4**	d4	P4	4d5	3d5	**dd5**	d5	P5
F♭♭	P1	A1	**AA1**	3A1	4A1	M2	A2	**AA2**	3A2	4A2	M3	A3	**AA3**	3A3	4A3	A4	AA4	**3A4**	4A4	5A4
F♭	d8	P1	**A1**	AA1	3A1	m2	M2	**A2**	AA2	3A2	m3	M3	**A3**	AA3	3A3	P4	A4	**AA4**	3A4	4A4
F	**dd8**	**d8**	**P1**	**A1**	**AA1**	**d2**	**m2**	**M2**	**A2**	**AA2**	**d3**	**m3**	**M3**	**A3**	**AA3**	**d4**	**P4**	**A4**	**AA4**	**3A4**
F#	3d8	dd8	**d8**	P1	A1	dd2	d2	**m2**	M2	A2	dd3	d3	**m3**	M3	A3	dd4	d4	**P4**	A4	AA4
Fx	4d8	3d8	**dd8**	d8	P1	3d2	dd2	**d2**	m2	M2	3d3	dd3	**d3**	m3	M3	3d4	dd4	**d4**	P4	A4
G♭♭	m7	M7	**A7**	AA7	3A7	P1	A1	**AA1**	3A1	4A1	M2	A2	**AA2**	3A2	4A2	M3	A3	**AA3**	3A3	4A3
G♭	d7	m7	**M7**	A7	AA7	d8	P1	**A1**	AA1	3A1	m2	M2	**A2**	AA2	3A2	m3	M3	**A3**	AA3	3A3
G	**dd7**	**d7**	**m7**	**M7**	**A7**	**dd8**	**d8**	**P1**	**A1**	**AA1**	**d2**	**m2**	**M2**	**A2**	**AA2**	**d3**	**m3**	**M3**	**A3**	**AA3**
G#	3d7	dd7	**d7**	m7	M7	3d8	dd8	**d8**	P1	A1	dd2	d2	**m2**	M2	A2	dd3	d3	**m3**	M3	A3
Gx	4d7	3d7	**dd7**	d7	m7	4d8	3d8	**dd8**	d8	P1	3d2	dd2	**d2**	m2	M2	3d3	dd3	**d3**	m3	M3
A♭♭	m6	M6	**A6**	AA6	3A6	m7	M7	**A7**	AA7	3A7	P1	A1	**AA1**	3A1	4A1	M2	A2	**AA2**	3A2	4A2
A♭	d6	m6	**M6**	A6	AA6	d7	m7	**M7**	A7	AA7	d8	P1	**A1**	AA1	3A1	m2	M2	**A2**	AA2	3A2
A	**dd6**	**d6**	**m6**	**M6**	**A6**	**dd7**	**d7**	**m7**	**M7**	**A7**	**dd8**	**d8**	**P1**	**A1**	**AA1**	**d2**	**m2**	**M2**	**A2**	**AA2**
A#	3d6	dd6	**d6**	m6	M6	3d7	dd7	**d7**	m7	M7	3d8	dd8	**d8**	P1	A1	dd2	d2	**m2**	M2	A2
Ax	4d6	3d6	**dd6**	d6	m6	4d7	3d7	**dd7**	d7	m7	4d8	3d8	**dd8**	d8	P1	3d2	dd2	**d2**	m2	M2
B♭♭	d5	P5	**A5**	AA5	3A5	m6	M6	**A6**	AA6	3A6	m7	M7	**A7**	AA7	3A7	P1	A1	**AA1**	3A1	4A1
B♭	dd5	d5	**P5**	A5	AA5	d6	m6	**M6**	A6	AA6	d7	m7	**M7**	A7	AA7	d8	P1	**A1**	AA1	3A1
B	**3d5**	**dd5**	**d5**	**P5**	**A5**	**dd6**	**d6**	**m6**	**M6**	**A6**	**dd7**	**d7**	**m7**	**M7**	**A7**	**dd8**	**d8**	**P1**	**A1**	**AA1**
B#	4d5	3d5	**dd5**	d5	P5	3d6	dd6	**d6**	m6	M6	3d7	dd7	**d7**	m7	M̃7	3d8	dd8	**d8**	P1	A1
Bx	5d5	4d5	**3d5**	dd5	d5	4d6	3d6	**dd6**	d6	m6	4d7	3d7	**dd7**	d7	m7̃	4d8	3d8	**dd8**	d8	P1

KEY: 3A = triple augmented AA = double augmented A = augmented P = Perfect
M = major m = minor d = diminished dd = double diminished 3d = triple diminished

Writing Intervals

Intervals are written using either of the two methods discussed for analysis. With either method the first step is to write the upper note according to the distance between the notes, without regard to quality. The second step is either to construct a major scale or to determine the number of half steps needed. Finally, the upper note is adjusted with accidentals, if necessary, to produce the required interval.

Example 1:

Given: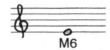

1. Write the upper note:

2. Construct a major scale on the lower note:

3. Adjust the upper note:
"C" is not a member of the E major scale, so the interval as written is a minor sixth. Raise the upper note one-half step to make a major sixth.

Example 2:

Given:

1. Write the upper note: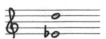

2. Find the number of half steps:
Extrapolating from the table (moving up on the chart from minor seventh) on page 118,
diminished seventh = 9 half steps.

3. Adjust the upper note:
9 half steps above "E-flat" is "C," or "D-double flat" enharmonically.

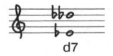

Inversion of Intervals

If the upper and lower notes of an interval are switched, the interval has been *inverted*.

Because of the mathematical relationship between an interval and its inversion, the quality of the inversion may be found from the following table.

INTERVAL	INVERSION
P1	P8
m2	M7
M2	m7
m3	M6
M3	m6
P4	P5
A4/d5	d5/A4
P5	P4
m6	M3
M6	m3
m7	M2
M7	m2
P8	P1

Augmented and diminished intervals, not shown except for the tritone, invert with one another just as the major and minor intervals invert with one another.

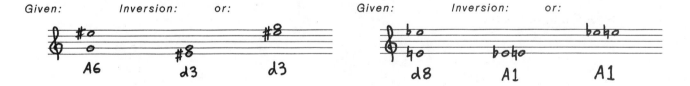

4. Triads

Most Western harmony is based on *tertian* harmony: the chords are formed by stacking intervals of thirds. A chord containing three notes is called a *triad*. Chords containing more than three notes are described by their largest interval. Triads will be discussed in this section; the triadic extensions (7th, 9th, 11th and 13th chords) will be discussed later.

Quality of Triads

The four types of triads used in Western music are the *augmented triad*, the *major triad*, the *minor triad*, and the *diminished triad*.

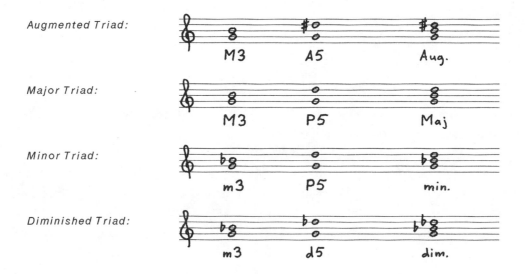

Inversion of Triads

The triad will not necessarily appear in its tertian form; the notes may be rearranged in various ways. If the root is the lowest pitch, regardless of the arrangement of the other pitches, the triad is in *root position*; if the third is the lowest pitch the triad is in *first inversion*; and if the fifth is the lowest pitch, the triad is in *second inversion*.

Triads in Root Position   *Triads in First Inversion*   *Triads in Second Inversion*

Harmonic Analysis of Triads

Two methods are used to describe triads. The first method, used for performance, describes the triad by giving the root and the quality; this method is described in chapter 3. The second method, more appropriate for theory, uses Roman numerals to describe both the quality and harmonic function of the triad in relation to the key of the music.

A capital Roman numeral describes a major triad and a small Roman numeral describes a minor triad. A "+" is added to a capital Roman numeral to describe an augmented triad, and a "o" is added to a small Roman numeral to describe a diminished triad. At the beginning of the analysis the key of the tonic triad is stated using a capital letter for a major key and a small letter for a minor key. The analysis of the triads of the major and minor scales follows:

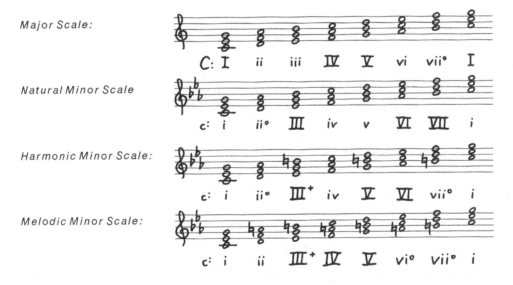

Major Scale: C: I   ii   iii   IV   V   vi   vii°   I

Natural Minor Scale   c: i   ii°   III   iv   v   VI   VII   i

Harmonic Minor Scale: c: i   ii°   III⁺   iv   V   VI   vii°   i

Melodic Minor Scale: c: i   ii   III⁺   IV   V   vi°   vii°   i

When using Roman numeral analysis, *figured bass* symbols are added following the Roman numeral to show the inversion of the chord. Figured bass symbols were developed during the Baroque to allow a keyboard player to play all the chords in a composition given only a cello part. The figures in figured bass describe the intervals above the bass note that are used in the chord.

By convention, the "5" and "3" are usually left out unless the intervals have been altered in some way. If a chord is altered, the accidental of the altered note is placed after the figured bass symbol. An accidental without a number applies to the third. A slash through a number means that the note is raised a half step. The following example illustrates a line of figured bass and the chords which the symbols represent.

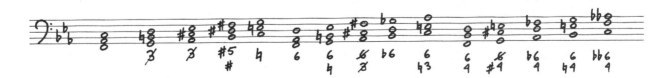

5. Four Part Writing

The underlying framework for Western music is based on *four part writing*. Basic four part writing, typical of hymns and chorales, is very mechanical in the guidelines and techniques used; nevertheless, it must be studied carefully before more complex forms of writing are attempted.

Four part music is written on the *grand staff* with the soprano and alto voices in the treble clef and the tenor and bass voices in the bass clef. The stems are split on each staff. If the tenor voice moves above middle C, the part is placed on ledger lines with respect to the bass clef staff. Likewise, the alto part is placed on ledger lines with respect to the treble clef staff if it drops below middle C.

Triads in Root Position

The guidelines for writing a triad in root position are as follows:

- When a triad is in root position, double the bass.

- Do not cross the voices (i.e. the alto may not be on a pitch higher than that of the soprano).

- The distance between the soprano and alto and between the alto and tenor should not be greater than one octave. The distance between the tenor and bass may exceed one octave.

A chord may be written in either *closed* or *open structure*. In closed structure the notes of the soprano, alto, and tenor are as close together as possible; there are no chord tones between the voices. In open structure the upper three voices are separated by one, and only one, chord tone.

Closed Structure: *Open Structure:*

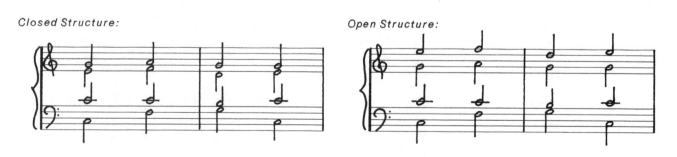

A melodic line is formed when triads are connected together in succession. The movement of voices from one chord to the next is called *voice leading*. Four kinds of motion may occur between two voices. *Similar motion* occurs when both voices move in the same direction but by different intervals. *Parallel motion* occurs when both voices move in the same direction by the same interval. *Oblique motion* occurs when one voice moves, but the other voice repeats the same note. *Contrary motion* occurs when the voices move in opposite directions. If the voices do not move, *repetition* has occurred.

Good voice leading takes place when the voices move smoothly without large leaps. The guidelines for connecting two triads in root position with good voice leading are as follows:

- If the two triads have common tones, retain them in the same voice and move the other voices to the nearest chord tones.

- If there are no common tones, then move the upper three voices in contrary motion to the bass to the nearest chord tones.

- Do not write leaps of an augmented second or augmented fourth.

- Avoid parallel motion of perfect unisons, perfect fifths, and perfect octaves.

- Avoid crossed voices.

The following example shows proper voice leading for triads in root position:

One exception to normal voice leading occurs when moving from the dominant to the submediant in harmonic minor. If normal voice leading is followed, the interval of an augmented second will occur because of the accidental in the dominant triad. To avoid the augmented second, double the third in the submediant chord.

Incorrect (doubled bass in VI chord):

Correct (doubled third in VI chord):

The error of *crossed voices* may occur in two ways. In a single chord if the voices are not distributed in order from high to low, the voices are crossed vertically. If one voice moves to a pitch lower than the voice below it just left, or if a voice moves to a pitch higher than the voice above it just left, the voices are crossed horizontally.

Vertically crossed voices:

Horizontally crossed voices:

Triads in First Inversion

Whenever a triad is written with the third in the bass, the triad is in first inversion. Triads in first inversion are used frequently to reduce the number of leaps in the bass line. They are not as stable as root position triads and can present some tricky voice leading problems when used several times in a row. The following guidelines apply to triads in first inversion.

- When a major or minor triad is in first inversion, double the soprano.

- When connecting a triad in first inversion to any other triad, move the doubled tones in similar, oblique, or contrary motion to the nearest chord tones. Next, move the remaining tones to the nearest note which gives proper doubling.

- Write diminished triads in first inversion with the bass doubled.

- Do not double the leading tone.

- Avoid parallel motion of perfect unisons, perfect fifths, and perfect octaves. Irregular doubling in some triads may be required when several first inversion triads are connected together.

Triads in Second Inversion

Second inversion triads are usually referred to as "six-four" chords. Because second inversion triads are unstable, they are usually not used except in one of the four traditional ways: the *cadential six-four*, the *passing six-four*, the *pedal six-four*, and the *arpeggio six-four*.

The cadential six-four occurs just before the final chord of the cadence on a strong beat. Usually, the tonic six-four is used; occasionally the subdominant six-four is written. The cadential six-four chords are correctly written and resolved with the bass doubled and two of the three upper voices moved down by step.

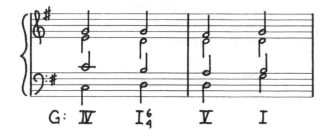

The passing six-four is placed between a triad in root position and the same triad in first inversion, or vice versa. Usually a dominant six-four is placed between two tonic triads, or a tonic six-four is placed between two subdominant triads.

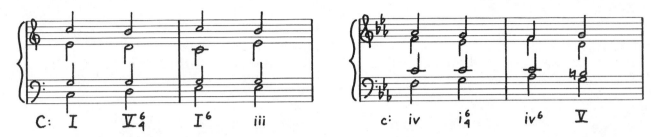

The pedal six-four is usually the subdominant six-four used between two tonic triads. It is called a pedal six-four because the bass note does not change.

The arpeggio six-four is a result of arpeggiating a chord in the bass voice.

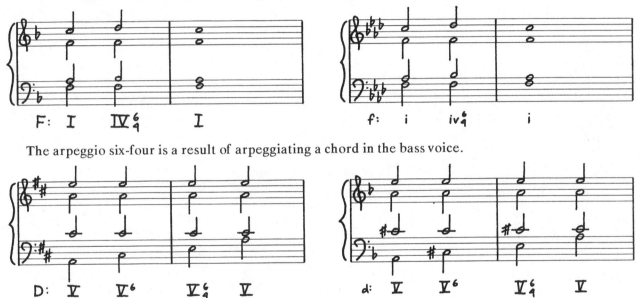

Harmonic Progression and Cadences

A series of chords is called a *harmonic progression*. If the movement from one chord to the next gives a sense of forward motion, the motion is called *progression*. Any other motion is called *retrogression*. Progression occurs when the interval from the root of one chord to the root of the next chord is down a fifth, down a third, or up a second. Root movement of up a fourth, up a sixth, or down a seventh is also progressive, because these intervals are the inversions of the fifth, third, and second. Most music contains both progression and retrogression. Progressive motion occurs between triads as follows:

- down a fifth: I IV vii° iii vi ii V I
- down a third: I vi IV ii vii° V iii I
- up a second: I ii iii IV V vi vii° I

The *primary triads*, the tonic, subdominant, and dominant, are used for the foundation of a harmonic progression. Any melody may be harmonized using only these three triads. To add variety to the harmony, *secondary triads* may be substituted for the primary triads.

Primary Triads	Related Secondary Triads
tonic (I)	submediant (vi)
subdominant (IV)	supertonic (ii)
dominant (V)	mediant (iii)
	leading tone (vii°)

The progression that brings a phrase to a close is called the *cadence*. The four common cadences are the *authentic cadence*, the *plagal cadence*, the *half cadence*, and the *deceptive cadence*. The cadential six-four chord may be added to any of these cadences.

Cadence	Chord Progression (major key)	(minor key)
Authentic	V - I vii° - I	V - i, V - I*, v - i, v - I* VII - i, VII - I*, vii° - i, vii° - I*
Plagal	IV - I	iv - i, iv - I*
Half	I - V IV - V ii - V	i - V, i - v iv - V, iv - v ii° - V, ii° - v
Deceptive	V - vi	V - VI, v - VI

*a raised third in the tonic triad to end a minor phrase with a major chord is called a Picardy Third.

A cadence is called *perfect* if both of the triads forming the cadence are in root position, and the bass is doubled in the soprano in the last triad. If both requirements are not fulfilled, the cadence is *imperfect*.

A special half cadence called the *phrygian cadence* occurs when the following requirements are met.

- Progression is from the subdominant to dominant in harmonic minor.

- The dominant triad is in root position with the bass doubled by the soprano.

- The bass and soprano voices move in contrary motion by step.

6. Nonharmonic Tones

Nonharmonic tones do not fit into the harmony of the chord progression. They are ornamental and produce dissonance.

NAME	DESCRIPTION	EXAMPLE
Passing Tone	Approached and left by step without a change in direction.	
Neighboring Tone	Approached and left by step with a change in direction.	
Changing Tones	Approached and left by step or leap, in opposite directions, usually between the same tones.	
Free Tone	Approached and left by leap.	
Appoggiatura	Approached by leap, left by step.	
Escape Tone	Approached by step, left by leap.	
Suspension	Approached by repetition, left by step.	
Anticipation	Approached by step, left by repetition.	
Pedal Tone	Usually a sustained bass note (on the organ pedals).	

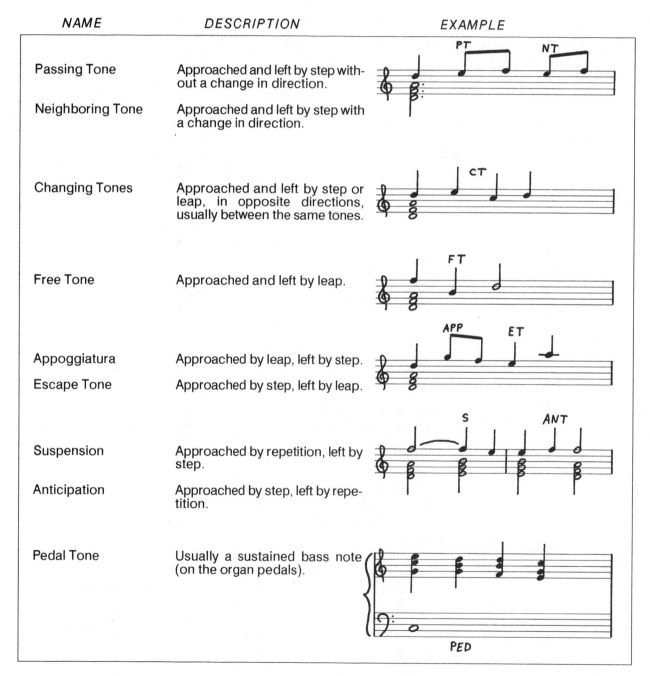

132

7. Seventh Chords

The *seventh chord* is formed by adding the interval of a seventh above the root to a triad. Because the interval of a seventh is dissonant, seventh chords are resolved to triads.

Quality of Seventh Chords

Seven different seventh chords are used in Western music:

Harmonic Analysis of Seventh Chords

Roman numeral analysis for seventh chords is as follows:

Two additional notations are used to distinguish two of the seventh chords in harmonic minor from their corresponding chords in the major scale. A slash through the "^{7}" shows that the seventh is raised one half step, forming a minor-major seventh chord. The notation "^{d7}" is added for a diminished-minor seventh chord.

Resolution of Seventh Chords

The most common seventh chord is the dominant seventh chord, a major-minor seventh chord. The major-minor seventh chord contains a tritone between the third and seventh and is usually resolved according to the following guidelines:

- If the tritone is an augmented fourth, resolve the voices outward to form a sixth.

- If the tritone is a diminished fifth, resolve the voices inward to form a third.

- Move the seventh down by step.

- Move the remaining tone to the nearest note. Irregular doubling may occur in the chord following the seventh chord.

- Avoid parallel perfect fifths, parallel perfect octaves, and crossed voices.

The leading tone seventh chord is also used frequently. In a major key there is a tritone between the root and fifth; in a minor key there is an additional tritone between the third and seventh. Try to resolve both tritones.

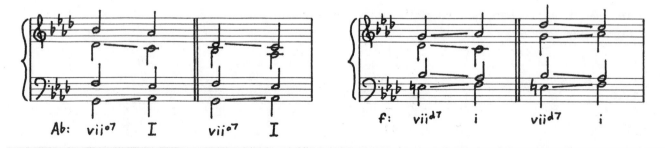

Use of Seventh Chords

The seventh chords, except the tonic seventh, serve the same harmonic function as the triads with which they are associated. The dominant and leading tone seventh chords are the most common chords. They usually resolve to the tonic triad.

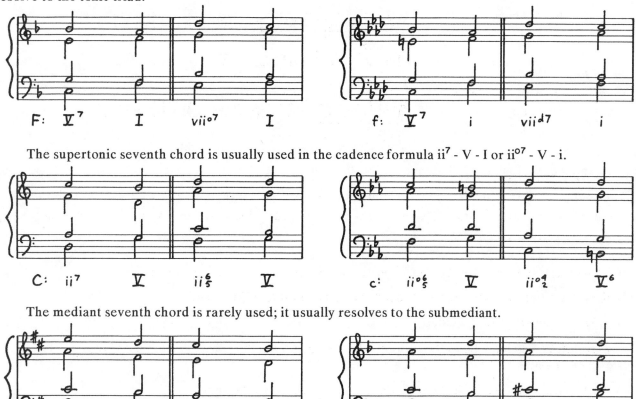

The supertonic seventh chord is usually used in the cadence formula ii⁷ - V - I or ii°⁷ - V - i.

The mediant seventh chord is rarely used; it usually resolves to the submediant.

The subdominant seventh usually resolves to the dominant or dominant seventh; occasionally it resolves to the supertonic.

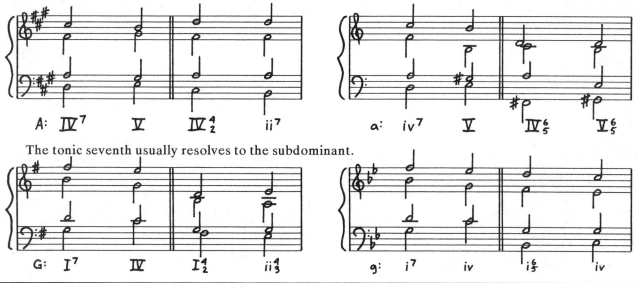

The tonic seventh usually resolves to the subdominant.

8. Altered Chords

Secondary Dominants

Secondary dominants are altered chords which act to embellish the major or minor triad which they precede. The secondary dominants are the dominant and leading tone triads and seventh chords of the key based on the root of the triad which it embellishes.

The secondary dominants of the mediant in C major are shown in the next example. (The chords are the dominant and leading tone triads and seventh chords in the key of E major and e minor, because "E" is the root of the mediant in C major.)

Secondary dominants have the same tritones as any other seventh chords and are resolved the same way.

Example 1:

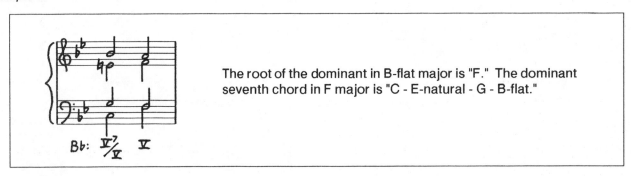

The root of the dominant in B-flat major is "F." The dominant seventh chord in F major is "C - E-natural - G - B-flat."

Example 2:

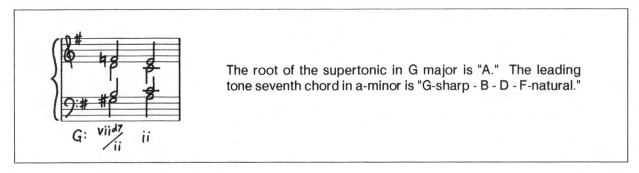

The root of the supertonic in G major is "A." The leading tone seventh chord in a-minor is "G-sharp - B - D - F-natural."

Example 3:

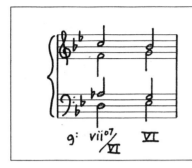

The root of the submediant in g minor is "E-flat." The leading tone seventh chord in E-flat major is "D - F - A-flat - C."

g: vii°⁷/VI   VI

Example 4:

The root of the subdominant in e minor is "A." The dominant triad in A minor is "E - G-sharp - B."

e: V/iv   iv

Augmented Sixth Cords

Augmented sixth chords are so named because they contain an interval of an augmented sixth. There are three types of augmented sixth chords: the *Italian sixth*, the *German sixth*, and the *French sixth*.

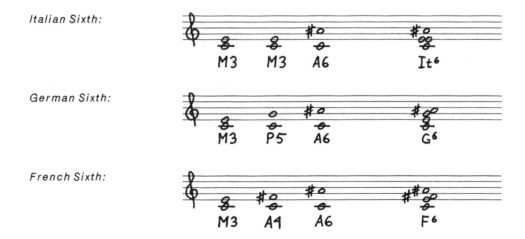

Italian Sixth: M3   M3   A6   It⁶

German Sixth: M3   P5   A6   G⁶

French Sixth: M3   A4   A6   F⁶

The augmented sixth chord is usually built on the sixth degree of the harmonic minor scale or on the lowered sixth degree of the major scale. It may also be built on the lowered second degree of the major or minor scale or on the fourth degree of the major scale.

When built on the sixth or lowered sixth degree, the augmented sixth chord usually resolves to the dominant triad or to the tonic triad in second inversion. When built on the lowered second degree or on the fourth degree, it usually resolves to the tonic triad in root position.

To resolve the augmented sixth chord, resolve the augmented sixth outward to an octave. Move the other tones to the nearest tones which give good voice leading. The German sixth will have parallel perfect fifths when resolved; do not write the parallel perfect fifths between the soprano and the bass.

Neapolitan Sixth Chords

The *neapolitan sixth chord* is a major triad built on the lowered second degree of the major or minor scale and used in first inversion with the bass doubled. It usually resolves to the dominant, sometimes by way of a secondary dominant, or by way of the tonic triad in second inversion.

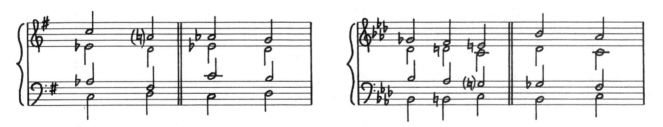

9. Ninth, Eleventh, and Thirteenth Chords

Ninth, eleventh, and thirteenth chords are usually built on the dominant, but they may also be found on the tonic and supertonic of the major scale or on the subdominant of the minor scale. Chords built on the dominant usually resolve to the tonic triad.

The dominant ninth chord in a major key is called a major ninth chord. It consists of a major-minor seventh chord and a major ninth. In a minor key, the ninth is minor and the chord is called a minor ninth chord.

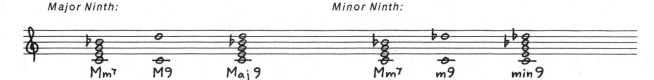

In four part writing, the dominant ninth is usually used in root position with the fifth omitted and the ninth at least one octave above the bass.

The dominant eleventh chord is a dominant ninth chord with an additional interval of a major eleventh above the bass. In four part writing, the third and fifth, or the third and ninth, are usually omitted.

The dominant thirteenth chord is the largest diatonic chord that may be written, as it contains every note of the scale. In four part writing the fifth, ninth, and eleventh are usually omitted. If the eleventh is retained, omit the third.

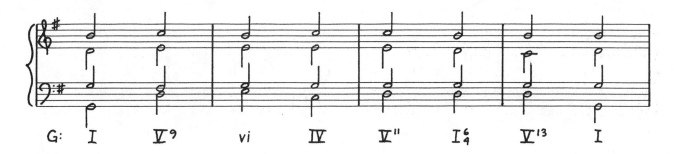

10. Modulation

Modulation occurs when the tonal center (key) of the music changes. A change of mode without a change of tonal center is not a modulation.

Most modulations are to a *relative key*. The relative keys of any given key are as follows:

- The relative major or minor.
- The relative major and minor of the dominant.
- The relative major and minor of the subdominant.

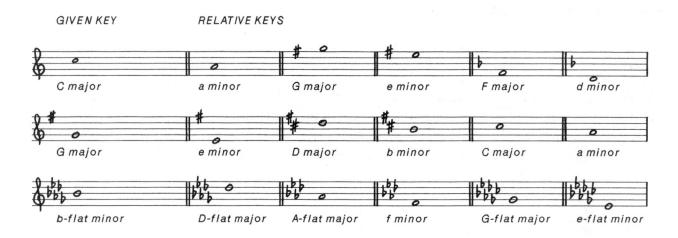

Basic modulations fall into three categories: *phrase modulations, common chord modulations*, and *chromatic modulations*.

Phrase Modulation

A phrase modulation occurs immediately following a cadence. The cadence provides a break, and the next phrase begins in the new key.

Common Chord Modulation

A common chord modulation occurs when the pivot from one key to another uses a chord common to both keys. The chord preceding the pivot chord is often a dominant, leading tone, or secondary dominant of the new key.

Chromatic Modulation

A chromatic modulation occurs when the key changes during chromatic motion, usually in the bass. There is usually no common chord between the two keys.

Appendix C
Dictionary of Musical Terms

Scales and Note Names

English	Italian	French	German
C	Do	Ut	C
D	Re	Re	D
E	Mi	Mi	E
F	Fa	Fa	F
G	Sol	Sol	G
A	La	La	A
B-flat	La-bemolle	La-bèmol	B
B	Si	Si	H
Flat	Bemolle	Bèmol	Es
Sharp	Diesis	Diéze	Is
Major	Maggiore	Mejeur	Dur
Minor	Minore	Mineur	Moll

Instruments

English	Italian	French	German
Piccolo	Flauto piccolo	Petite Flûte	Kleine Flöte
Flute	Flauto	Grande Flûte	Grosse Flöte
Oboe	Oboe	Hautbois	Hoboe
English Horn	Corno Inglese	Cor Anglais	Englisch Horn
Clarinet	Clarinetto	Clarinette	Klarinette
Bassoon	Fagotto	Bassoon	Fagott
Saxophone	Sassofono	Saxophone	Saxophon
Horn	Corno	Cor	Horn
Trumpet	Tromba	Trompette	Trompete
Cornet	Cornetto a pistoni	Cornet-á-pistons	Cornette
Trombone	Trombone	Trombone	Posaune
Baritone	Baritono	Baritone	Baryton
Tuba	Tuba	Tuba	Tuba
Violin	Violino	Violon	Violine
Viola	Viola	Alto	Bratsche
Cello	Violoncello	Violoncelle	Violoncello
Bass	Contrabasso	Contrebasse	Kontrabass
Harp	Arpa	Harpe	Harfe
Celesta	Celesta	Cèlesta	Celeste
Harpsichord	Clavicembalo	Clavecin	Kielfugel
Organ	Organo	Orgue	Orgel
Piano	Pianoforte	Piano	Klavier

Instruments (continued)

English	Italian	French	German
Timpani	Timpani	Timbales	Pauken
Snare Drum	Tamburo militaire	Tambour militare	Kleine Trommel
Bass Drum	Gran Cassa	Grosse Caisse	Grosse Trommel
Cymbals	Piatti	Cymbales	Becken
Tambourine	Tamburino	Tambour de basque	Tamburin
Triangle	Triangolo	Triangle	Triangel
Castanets	Castagnette	Castagnettes	Kastagnetten
Chimes	Campagne	Cloches	Glocken
Bells	Campanelli	Carillon	Glockenspiel
Xylophone	Xylophono	Xylophone	Xylophon
Vibraphone	Vibrafono	Vibraphone	Vibraphon
Marimba	Marimba	Marimba	Marimba
Soprano	Soprano	Soprano	Sopran
Alto	Alto	Contralto	Alt
Tenor	Tenore	Tènor	Tenor
Baritone	Baritono	Baritone	Baryton
Bass	Basso	Basse	Bass

Performance Directions

English	Italian	French	German
with mute	con sordino	avec sordine	mit Dämpfer
without mute	senza sordino	sanz sordine	ohne Dämpfer
open	arpeuto	ouvert	offen
stopped	chiuso	bouchè	gestopft
brassy	chiuse	cuivrè	schmetternd
plucked	pizzacato	--	--
with the wood	col legno	--	--
at the bridge	sul ponticello	sur le chevalet	am Steg
over the fingerboard	sul tasto	sur la touche	am Griffbrett
at the point of the bow	apunte d'arco	an pointe d'archet	ander spitze
ordinary way	modo ordinario	mode ordinaire	gewöhnlich
change from X to Y	X muta in Y	changez X en Y	X nach Y umstimmen
all	tutti	tout	alle
unison (a2)	unisono (a2)	unis (á2)	einfach (zu2)
divided	divisi	divisè	geteilt

Dynamics

English	Italian
as soft as possible	pianississimo (*ppp*)
very soft	pianissimo (*pp*)
soft	piano (*p*)
moderately soft	mezzo piano (*mp*)
moderately loud	mezzo forte (*mf*)
loud	forte (*f*)
very loud	fortissimo (*ff*)
as loud as possible	fortississimo (*fff*)
forced accent	sfortzando (*sfz*)
loud, then suddenly soft	forte piano (*fp*)
suddenly (suddenly loud)	subito (*sub. f*)
gradually increase in volume	crescendo (*cresc.*)
gradually decrease in volume	diminuendo (*dim.*)
little by little	poco a poco

Tempo

English	Italian
very fast	presto
fast	allegro
moderately fast	allegretto
moderate tempo	moderato
faster than andante	andantino
walking tempo	andante
slow (mournfully)	lento
slow (expressive)	largo
slower than largo	larghetto
very slow (solemn)	grave
gradually increase in speed	accelerando (*accel.*)
gradually decrease in speed	rallentando (*rall.*)
gradually decrease in speed	ritardando (*rit.*)
little by little	poco a poco
immediately slower	ritenuto (*riten.*)
slowing down	allegrando
resume tempo	a tempo
the same tempo	l'istesso tempo
the first tempo	tempo primo, tempo I
suddenly faster	stretto
gradually faster and faster	stringendo (*string.*)

Dictionary of Foreign Terms

A

A (It), by
Abandonnè (Fr), free
Abbando (It), with abandon
Absetzen (Gr), separated
A capella (It), unaccompanied
Accusè (Fr), with emphasis
Ad libitum (Latin), at will
Affabile (It), gentle
Affannato (It), excited
Affetuoso (It), affectionate
Affretando (It), hurrying
Agevole (It), easy
Agiatamente (It), with ease
Agilmente (It), with agility
Agitado (It), agitated
Agitato (It), excited
Agitè (Fr), agitated
A la (Fr), to the
Al fine (It), to the end
Alla (It), in the style of
Alle breve (It), cut time
Al segno (It), to the sign
Amabile (It), amiable
Amorevole (It), amiable
Amoroso (It), amorous
Ancora (It), once more
Anfang (Gr), beginning
Angoscioso (It), sorrowful
Animato (It), animated
Animè (Fr), animated
Anmutig (Gr), graceful
Anschwellen (Gr), increase
A piacere (It), at will
Appassionato (It), with passion
Appoggiando (It), emphasized
Appoggiato (It), dwelt upon
Appuyè (Fr), with emphasis
Arditamente (It), boldly
Ardore (It), warmth
Ariosa (It), songlike
Assai (It), very
Assez (Fr), enough
Attaca (It), no pause

Aufgeregt (Gr), excited
Ausdruck (Gr), expression
Aussi (Fr), also
Avec (Fr), with

B

Battuta (It), beat
Bedächtig (Gr), deliberate
Behaglich (Gr), with ease
Behende (Gr), nimbly
Belebend (Gr), animated
Ben (It), will
Beruhigt (Gr), calm
Bestimmt (Gr), with decision
Betont (Gr), emphasized
Bewegt (Gr), animated
Bien (Fr), will
Bravura (It), bold
Breit (Gr), broad
Brillante (It), brilliant
Brio (It), spirit

C

Cadenza (It), an extended embellishment
Calando (It), softer and slower
Calmando (It), quieting
Calore (It), warmth
Cantabile (It), singing
Capriccio a (It), at pleasure
Ce'dez (Fr), slower
Celere (It), quick
Chaleur (Fr), warmth
Coda (It), ending
Col (It), with
Colla (It), with the
Comado (It), easily
Come (It), like
Comodo (It), comfortable
Con (It), with
Concitato (It), excited

D

Da Capo (It), from the beginning
Dal Segno (It), from the sign

Dictionary of Foreign Terms (continued)

Decidè (Fr), decided
Deciso (It), decided
Dehors (Fr), emphasized
Delicato (It), delicate
Delore (It), grief
Derb (Gr), rough
Deutlich (Gr), distinct
Diluendo (It), fading away
Dolce (It), sweetly
Dolcissimo (It), very sweetly
Dolente (It), sorrowful
Doloroso (It), sorrowful
Doppio (It), double
Douce (Fr), sweet
Doucement (Fr), gently
Douleur (Fr), sorrow
Douloureux (Fr), sorrowful
Duramente (It), harshly

E
E (It), and
Éclatant (Fr), brilliant
Eilend (Gr), hurrying
Elan (Fr), dash
Elegante (It), with ease
Empfindung (Gr), feeling
Empressè (Fr), hurrying
Ému (Fr), with feeling
Enchaînement (Fr), no pause
Energico (It), energetic
Erlöschend (Gr), fading away
Ermattend (Gr), tiring
Ernst (Gr), serious
Ersterbend (Gr), fading away
Espressione (It), expression
Espressivo (It), expressively
Estinto (It), barely audible
Éteint (Fr), barely audible
Etwas (Gr), somewhat
Expressif (Fr), expressive

F
Facilement (Gr), easily
Facilimente (It), easily
Fastoso (It), pompous
Feierlich (Gr), solemn
Feroce (It), ferocious
Fervore (It), fervor

Festoso (It), festive
Fiero (It), spirited
Finale (It), the last section
Fine (It), the end
Flebile (It), mournful
Fliessend (Gr), flowing
Flüssig (Gr), flowing
Frei (Gr), free
Frettoloso (It), hurried
Fröhlich (Gr), joyful
Fuoco (It), fire

G
Gai (Fr), gay
Gaiment (Fr), gaily
Garbato (It), graceful
Gebunden (Gr), smooth
Gefühlvoll (Gr), with feeling
Gehalten (Gr), sustained
Gelassen (Gr), calm
Gemächlich (Gr), comfortable
Gemendo (It), lamenting
Gemessen (Gr), restrained
Genend (Gr), walking
Gesangvoll (Gr), songlike
Geschwing (Gr), quick
Getragen (Gr), sustained
Giocoso (It), humorous
Gioioso (It), joyous
Giusto (It), correct
Goicoso (It), playful
Gracieux (Fr), graceful
Graderole (It), pleasing
Gradevole (It), pleasant
Grandezza (It), grandeur
Grandioso (It), grand
Grazia (It), grace
Grazioso (It), graceful
Gtrepitoso (It), noisy
Guisto (It), in strict time
Gusto (It), zest

H
Hastig (Gr), hurrying
Heiter (Gr), cheerful
Hinsterbend (Gr), fading away
Hurtig (Gr), agile

Dictionary of Foreign Terms (continued)

I

Immer (Gr), always
Impetuoso (It), impetuously
Incalzando (It), hurrying
Indeciso (It), undecided
Innig (Gr), tender
Intrepido (It), bold

K

Klagend (Gr), lamenting
Kräftig (Gr), vigorous

L

Lagnoso (It), lamenting
Lancio (It), vigor
Larcrimoso (It), mournful
Largamente (It), broadly
Lebendig (Gr), lively
Lebhaft (Gr), lively
Legato (It), smooth
Le'germent (Fr), lightly
Leggiero (It), light
Licenza (It), liberty
Lieblich (Gr), sweet
Lieto (It), gay
Lievo (It), light
Liscio (It), even
L'istesso (It), the same
Loco (It), in place
Lourd (Gr), heavy
Lusingando (It), coaxing
Lustig (Gr), gay
Luttuoso (It), mournful

M

Ma (It), but
Maestoso (It), majestic
Marcato (It), marked
Markiert (Gr), marked
Markig (Gr), vigorous
Marquè (Fr), marked
Marziale (It), marchlike
Mässig (Gr), moderate
Meno (It), less
Mesto (It), sad
Mezzo (It), half
Mit (Gr), with
Moderato (It), moderate

Moderè (Fr), moderate
Molto (It), very
Morbido (It), smooth
Morendo (It), dying away
Mosso (It), motion
Moto (It), motion
Munter (Gr), cheerful

N

Nachlassend (Gr), relaxing
Nicht (Gr), not
Non (It), not

O

Ossia (It), or (easier part)

P

Pacato (It), calm
Parlando (It), like speech
Patetico (It), with emotion
Pathetisch (Gr), with emotion
Pen (Fr), little
Perdendo (It), dying away
Perdendosi (It), dying away
Pesante (It), heavy
Peu (Fr), little
Piacerole (It), agreeable
Piacevole (It), pleasing
Pianamente (It), smoothly
Pieno (It), full
Piu (It), more
Placido (It), calm
Plus (Fr), more
Poco (It), little
Poi (It), after
Pomposo (It), pompous
Pressante (It), hurrying
Pressez (Fr), hurrying
Primo (It), first

Q

Quasi (It), almost

R

Rasch (Gr), quick
Rattenuto (It), holding back
Ravvivando (It), quickening
Religioso (It), religious

Dictionary of Foreign Terms (continued)

Renforcer (Fr), reinforcing
Retenant (Fr), holding back
Rinforzando (It), reinforcing
Risoluto (It), boldly
Rubato (It), flexible tempo
Ruhig (Gr), quiet

S

Sanft (Gr), gentle
Scherzando (It), playful
Scherzhaft (Gr), playful
Schleppend (Gr), dragging
Schnell (Gr), quick
Schwindend (Gr), dying away
Schwungvoll (Gr), animated
Sciolto (It), unrestrained
Scucito (It), unconnected
Secco (It), dry
Seelenvoll (Gr) soulful
Segue (It), no pause
Sehr (Gr), very
Semplice (It), simple
Sempre (It), always
Sentito (It), expressive
Senza (It), without
Sereno (It), serene
Sforzando (It), forced
Sforzato (It), forcing
Simile (It), similar
Smorzando (It), dying away
Solennel (Fr), solemn
Sospirando (It), sighing
Sostenuto (It), sustained
Sotto (It), under
Sotto voce (It), subdued tone
Soupirant (Fr), sighing
Soutenu (Fr), sustained
Spianato (It), smooth
Spiritoso (It), spirited
Staccato (It), separated
Stentando (It), laboring
Sterbend (Gr), dying away

Subito (It), suddenly
Suivez (Fr), follow

T

Tacet (Latin), is silent
Tanto (It), so much
Teneramente (It), tenderly
Tenuto (It), hold to full value
Tranquillo (It), tranquil
Trascinando (It), dragging
Trattenuto (It), held back
Traurig (Gr), sad
Treibend (Gr), hurrying
Très (Fr), very
Troppo (It), too much

U

Un (Fr), a
Und (Gr), and
Unruhig (Gr), restless

V

Veloce (It), fast
Verhallend (Gr), fading away
Vif (Fr), lively
Vigoroso (It), vigorous
Vigoureux (Fr), vigorous
Vite (Fr), quick
Vivace (It), lively
Vivement (Fr), lively
Volante (It), rushing
Volti Subito (It), turn page quickly

W

Wärme (Gr), warmth
Wehmütg (Gr), sad
Wuchtig (Gr), forceful
Würdig (Gr), stately

Z

Zart (Gr), tender
Zeitmass (Gr), tempo

Reverse Dictionary of Foreign Terms
English to Italian

A

Affectionate, *affetuoso*
After, *poi*
Agitated, *agitado*
Agreeable, *piacerole*
Almost, *quasi*
Always, *sempre*
Amiable, amorevole, *amabile*
Amorous, *amoroso*
An extended embellishment, *cadenza*
And, *e*
Animated, *animato*
At will, *a piacere*
At pleasure, *capriccio a*

B

Barely audible, *estinto*
Beat, *battuta*
Bold, *intrepido, bravura*
Boldly, *risoluto, arditamente*
Brilliant, *brillante*
Broadly, *largamente*
But, *ma*
By, *a*

C

Calm, pacato, *placido*
Coaxing, *lusingando*
Comfortable, *comodo*
Correct, *giusto*
Cut time, *alle breve*

D

Decided, *deciso*
Delicate, *delicato*
Double, *doppio*
Dragging, *trascinando*
Dry, *secco*
Dwelt upon, *appoggiato*
Dying away, *morendo, perdendosi, perdendo,*
 smorzando

E

Easily, *facilimente, comado*

Easy, *agevole*
Emphasized, *appoggiando*
Ending, *coda*
Energetic, *energico*
Even, *liscio*
Excited, *concitato, affannato, agitato*
Expression, *espressione*
Expressive, *sentito*
Expressively, *espressivo*

F

Fading away, *diluendo*
Fast, *veloce*
Ferocious, *feroce*
Fervor, *fervore*
Festive, *festoso*
Fire, *fuoco*
First, *primo*
Flexible tempo, *rubato*
Forced, *sforzando*
Forcing, *sforzato*
From the beginning, *da Capo*
From the sign, *dal Segno*
Full, *pieno*

G

Gay, *lieto*
Gentle, *affabile*
Grace, *grazia*
Graceful, *grazioso, garbato*
Grand, *grandioso*
Grandeur, *grandezza*
Grief, *delore*

H

Half, *mezzo*
Harshly, *duramente*
Heavy, *pesante*
Held back, *trattenuto*
Hold to full value, *tenuto*
Holding back, *rattenuto*
Humorous, *giocoso*
Hurried, *frettoloso*
Hurrying, *affretando, incalzando, pressante*

Reverse Dictionary of Foreign Terms (English to Italian)

I

Impetuously, *impetuoso*
In place, *loco*
In strict time, *guisto*
In the style of, *alla*

J

Joyous, *gioioso*

L

Laboring, *stentando*
Lamenting, *lagnoso, gemendo*
Less, *meno*
Liberty, *licenza*
Light, *leggiero, lievo*
Like speech, *parlando*
Like, *come*
Little, *poco*
Lively, *vivace*

M

Majestic, *maestoso*
Marchlike, *marziale*
Marked, *marcato*
Moderate, *moderato*
More, *piu*
Motion, *moto, mosso*
Mournful, *flebile, larcrimoso, luttuoso*

N

No pause, *attaca, segue*
Noisy, *gtrepitoso*
Not, *non*

O

Once more, *ancora*
Or (easier part), *ossia*

P

Playful, *goicoso, scherzando*
Pleasant, *gradevole*
Pleasing, *piacevole, graderole*
Pompous, *fastoso, pomposo*

Q

Quick, *celere*
Quickening, *ravvivando*

Quieting, *calmando*

R

Reinforcing, *rinforzando*
Religious, *religioso*
Rushing, *volante*

S

Sad, *mesto*
Separated, *staccato*
Serene, *sereno*
Sighing, *sospirando*
Similar, *simile*
Simple, *semplice*
Singing, *cantabile*
Smooth, *morbido, legato, spianato*
Smoothly, *pianamente*
So much, *tanto*
Softer and slower, *calando*
Songlike, *ariosa*
Sorrowful, *dolente, doloroso, angoscioso*
Spirit, *brio*
Spirited, *spiritoso, fiero*
Subdued tone, *sotto voce*
Suddenly, *subito*
Sustained, *sostenuto*
Sweetly, *dolce*

T

Tenderly, *teneramente*
The last section, *finale*
The same, *l'istesso*
The end, *fine*
To the sign, *al segno*
To the end, *al fine*
Too much, *troppo*
Tranquil, *tranquillo*
Turn page quickly, *volti subito*

U

Unaccompanied, *a capella*
Unconnected, *scucito*
Undecided, *indeciso*
Under, *sotto*
Unrestrained, *sciolto*

V

Very sweetly, *dolcissimo*

Reverse Dictionary of Foreign Terms (English to Italian)

Very, *molto, assai*
Vigor, *lancio*
Vigorous, *vigoroso*

W
Warmth, *calore, ardore*
Will, *ben*
With emotion, *patetico*
With ease, *agiatamente, elegante*

With the, *colla*
With agility, *agilmente*
With passion, *appassionato*
With, *col, con*
With abandon, *abbando*
Without, *senza*

Z
Zest, *gusto*

Reverse Dictionary of Foreign Terms
English to French

A
A, *un*
Agitated, *agitè*
Also, *aussi*
Animated, *animè*

B
Barely audible, *éteint*
Brilliant, *éclatant*

D
Dash, *elan*
Decided, *decidè*

E
Emphasized, *dehors*
Enough, *assez*
Expressive, *expressif*

F
Follow, *suivez*
Free, *abandonnè*

G
Gaily, *gaiment*
Gay, *gai*
Gently, *doucement*
Graceful, *gracieux*

H
Holding back, *retenant*
Hurrying, *pressez, empressè*

L
Lightly, *le'germent*
Little, *pen, peu*
Lively, *vif, vivement*

M
Marked, *marquè*
Moderate, *moderè*
More, *plus*

N
No pause, *enchaînement*

Q
Quick, *vite*

R
Reinforcing, *renforcer*

S
Sighing, *soupirant*
Slower, *ce'dez*
Solemn, *solennel*
Sorrow, *douleur*
Sorrowful, *douloureux*
Sustained, *soutenu*
Sweet, *douce*

T
To the, *a la*

V
Very, *très*
Vigorous, *vigoureux*

W
Warmth, *chaleur*
Will, *bien*
With, *avec*
With feeling, *ému*
With emphasis, *appuyè, accusè*

Reverse Dictionary of Foreign Terms
English to German

A
Agile, *hurtig*
Always, *immer*
And, *und*
Animated, *belebend, schwungvoll, bewegt*

B
Beginning, *anfang*
Broad, *breit*

C
Calm, *beruhigt, gelassen*
Cheerful, *heiter, munter*
Comfortable, *gemächlich*

D
Deliberate, *bedächtig*
Distinct, *deutlich*
Dragging, *schleppend*
Dying away, *schwindend, sterbend*

E
Easily, *facilement*
Emphasized, *betont*
Excited, *aufgeregt*
Expression, *ausdruck*

F
Fading away, *hinsterbend, ersterbend,
 verhallend, erlöschend*
Feeling, *empfindung*
Flowing, *fliessend, flüssig*
Forceful, *wuchtig*
Free, *frei*

G
Gay, *lustig*
Gentle, *sanft*
Graceful, *anmutig*

H
Heavy, *lourd*
Hurrying, *hastig, eilend, treibend*

I
Increase, *anschwellen*

J
Joyful, *fröhlich*

L
Lamenting, *klagend*
Lively, *lebhaft, lebendig*

M
Marked, *markiert*
Moderate, *mässig*

N
Nimbly, *behende*
Not, *nicht*

P
Playful, *scherzhaft*

Q
Quick, *rasch, geschwing, schnell*
Quiet, *ruhig*

R
Relaxing, *nachlassend*
Restless, *unruhig*
Restrained, *gemessen*
Rough, *derb*

S
Sad, *wehmütig, traurig*
Separated, *absetzen*
Serious, *ernst*
Smooth, *gebunden*
Solemn, *feierlich*
Somewhat, *etwas*
Songlike, *gesangvoll*
Soulful, *seelenvoll*
Stately, *würdig*
Sustained, *gehalten, getragen*
Sweet, *lieblich*

Reverse Dictionary of Foreign Terms (English to German)

T
Tempo, *zeitmass*
Tender, *zart, innig*
Tiring, *ermattend*

V
Very, *sehr*
Vigorous, *markig, kräftig*

W
Walking, *genend*
Warmth, *wärme*
With, *mit*
With decision, *bestimmt*
With ease, *behaglich*
With emotion, *pathetisch*
With feeling, *gefühlvoll*

Index

Order additional copies of
Preparing Traditional Music Manuscript
direct from the publisher.

Preparing Traditional Music Manuscript, Including a Handbook of Instrumentation, Theory, and Musical Terms, Second Edition, by Michael Mohn. 176-page trade paperback. Index. ISBN 0-9624986-0-2. $22.50 (20% discount on two or more copies), no shipping charge on prepaid orders. M. Mohn Publishing, 2791F North Texas St., Suite 317, Fairfield, CA 94533-7308.

— — — — — — — — — — — — — — — — — — — —

Please send me _____ copies of *Preparing Traditional Music Manuscript*. I have enclosed $22.50 for one copy, or $18.00 per copy for two or more copies. (CA residents add 6.25% sales tax) Allow 30 days for delivery.

Name _____

Address _____

City _____ State _____ Zip _____

My check or money order, payable to M.Mohn Publishing, in the amount of $_____ is enclosed. Mail to:

M.Mohn Publishing
2791F North Texas St., Suite 317
Fairfield, CA 94533-7308

Sonata for unaccompained violin, by J. S. Bach.

ISBN: 0-9624986-0-2